Crosswinds

A cross-country bike ride that revealed why Canada is worth fighting for.

Doug Firby

BIG
LONELY
DOUG

ISBN: 978-1-0694355-0-7

Cover design by: Art Painter
Library of Congress Control Number: 2018675309
Printed in the United States of America

CONTENTS

DEDICATIONS

This book urges you to sign up to donate their organs for transplant. Lisa and Doug's son-in-law, Dax, would not be alive today were it not for the gift of life from someone whose name we will never know. To learn where you can register, click here: (https://www.canada.ca/en/health-canada/services/healthy-living/blood-organ-tissue-donation.html).

Each year, an average of 74 cyclists in Canada die in collisions. The Ledernier Velofantôme (Last Ghost Bike Campaign) raises funds for Advocacy for Respect for Cyclists, in Toronto, and Vélo Fantôme does the same in Montreal. Both organizations erect all-white bicycles as memorials for cyclists killed or hit while riding.

This book is also dedicated to Jay Austin. He, his partner Lauren Geoghegan, and two cyclists from Switzerland and the Netherlands were murdered in an ISIS-controlled section of Tajikistan in July 2018 during a world cycling tour. Read more about Jay's story at: SimplyJayAustin.com.

> *'I could die doing what I love, but I could also die never having really lived. To me, that would have been a far greater tragedy.'*
>
> *- Jay Austin*

FORWARD

COMMENTS FROM SOCIAL MEDIA AND FROM CONVERSATIONS WHEN PEOPLE LEARNED WE WERE CYCLING ACROSS CANADA:

Amazing!

Travel safe

Continued good health and kindness in your unbelievable journey

You guys rock!

Be safe out there!

So very cool!!

What an accomplishment

Super proud of them!!

Congratulations, what a ride!!!!

That's awesome! Congrats!! So proud of all of you!

So in awe of you and cannot wait to hear stories when you return

You're definitely badasses!!

What an amazing adventure. You guys are amazing!

What an epic trip!

Love following your journey

What a great experience for you!

Fantastic!! Okay way to go.

I love this.

Incredible guys

You are so inspiring!

So incredible!

I hate camping in the rain.

Wow. That looks so miserable!

How do you expect to get a tan in that? No! #besafe

Crykee!!!

I cannot believe you rode your flipping bike there from BC! You guys are all amazing! Enjoy Newfoundland!

Holy moly, macanannoli!

Way to go guys! You've inspired us all!!!

You missed a stat: how many beers?

Wowza! So so so proud and amazed by this journey!

What an bc accomplishment. ... and congrats to all the cyclists on that journey of Hope.

AWESOME ! Stay safe.

I'm floored at what you have accomplished.

Living the dream!!!

Or you could just kill yourself. Okay...maybe I'm missing something.

Are they mentally ill?

How bored do you have to be to want to ride your bikes across Canada?

PROLOGUE:

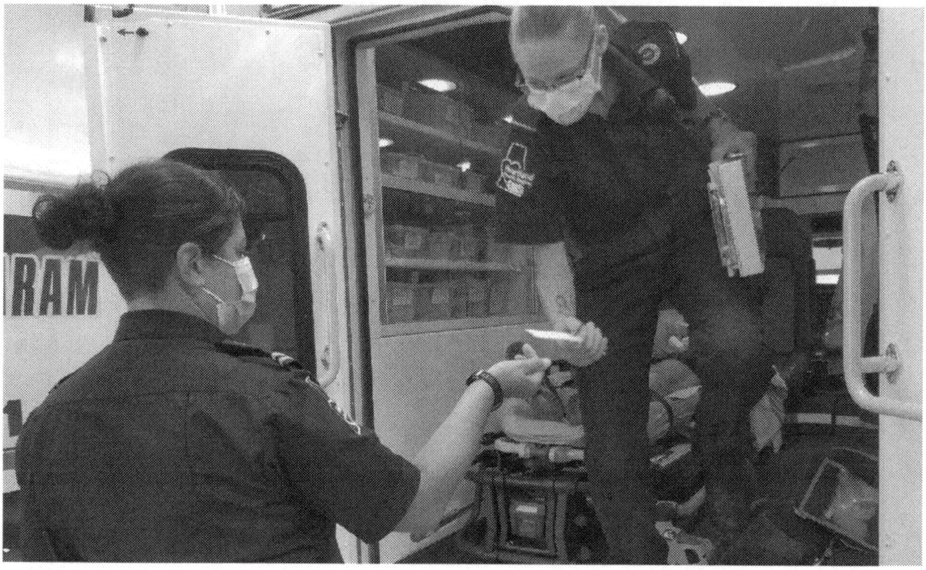

She lay dead still, splayed out on the searing pavement under the expansive azure Saskatchewan sky. Her eyes were wide open but she was clearly unconscious, or worse. Her cracked helmet half off her head. A trickle of saliva running out of her mouth and down her cheek.

When you ride your bicycle on public roads – which are, after all, designed for two-tonne hunks of metal and not for us – there are always dangers. We knew that. We knew every day can be a crap shoot. Still, nothing had prepared us for the moment in which one member of our close team of riders – and my partner for more than two decades – would be catastrophically injured.

Is this where our ambitious, some would say foolish, project to travel across the country by bike, reconnecting with Canadians, would end? In heartbreak and tragedy an hour's drive from the closest hospital? Surrounded by Saskatchewan's wheat and canola fields and a slowly building group of onlookers, their faces folded in grave creases?

Every dark possibility raced through my mind. It was an impossible twist in what had been a carefree and joyful experience. So many adventures had happened and we were looking forward to so many more. Now, it appeared a year-and-a-half of planning had led to a gut-wrenching end. All the abstract chatter about risks and common sense, now a jolting reality.

1. SOMETIMES A GREAT NOTION

DEPARTUS INTERRUPTUS

A lot of things happened in May 2021. Here are few of them:

The world was already more than a year into the coronavirus pandemic, and India was the first country to record more than 400,000 new cases – and 4,000 deaths – in one day.

Argentine news channel Chanal 26 reported that English

playwright William Shakespeare died after receiving a COVID-19 vaccine (missing his actual death date by 406 years).

A girls' school in Kabul was bombed, killing 85 and injuring hundreds more.

Multiple Israel air strikes in the Gaza Strip took dozens of lives.

A Malian woman gave birth to nonuplets in Morocco. That's nine babies, only the third such event in recorded history.

A cable car crashed in Italy, killing more than a dozen people.

Four MLB pitchers threw no-hitters.

The remains of 215 children were found buried on the grounds of the Kamloops Indian Residential School.

Brazilian Hélio Castroneves won the Indianapolis 500 for the fourth time.

And four cycling adventurists jumped into a red GMC Canyon pickup truck in Calgary and headed west to start a cross-Canada tour of discovery.

You can decide which of these events was the most noteworthy and transformative. The cyclists, an amorphous group calling itself ConnecTour, were pretty sure it would be us. Because we were on a mission, not to prove something but to discover something – about ourselves, about our country, about human nature and about a moment in time.

Yes, we were planning to ride our bicycles across the entire country, and not in a direct line, by the way, but via a rambling route that would total 8,749 kilometres spread over 102 days of frigid cold, driving rain, searing heat and relentless headwinds.

(Oh yes, there were many, many perfect days, too.) But we weren't setting out to set any speed records. Chris Bruckner, of Inuvik, NWT, did that in 2019, crossing the country in 13 days, three hours and 49 minutes. Bet he missed some of the highlights we took in. And we weren't out to sell a brand of bicycle or equipment, although most of us got very, very attached to our Surly Long Haul Truckers.

We were heading out to connect. With anyone who was curious enough to stop and say hello. With mayors. With shopkeepers. With retirees. With Indigenous people. With cops. With oil field workers and fruit growers and brewers and painters and carpenters and anyone else who was willing to take a few minutes or a few hours to build a bond with people they had just met.

Because – after 14 months of COVID-19 isolation and fear – we all felt a craving to rediscover a sense of community, to just talk to people about anything that was on their minds and to rebuild the connective tissue we had lost duringthis surrealistic moment in 21st century history. And we figured the best way to do that was at the speed of life, on a two-wheeled bike loaded down with 25 kilograms of gear, grinding up and sailing down mountain passes, fighting loose gravel on the dysfunctional Trans Canada Trail, reaching dead ends on logging roads and playing Russian roulette with SUVs on shoulderless paved two-lane roads.

We would put ourselves at the mercy of our own resourcefulness, the kindness of strangers and, the most unpredictable factor of them all: fate. Fate, it turns out, was more than kind to us on most days, although not all.

In that little red pickup truck that day on May 28th, 2021, were three people: Jennifer Herring, Rick McFerrin and me. Lisa Monforton, my wife, was to join us in Kelowna after visiting her daughter and son-in-law in Victoria. Jenn – who we quickly nicknamed Double-N Jenn – is young, in her 20s, and heading out for her first long-distance ride. She's not planning to go the distance, but rather ride from Victoria back to home in Calgary.

From left, Jenn, Rick, Lisa, Doug

Rick, our group leader, has a jaw-dropping record of bicycle touring experience. He and his partner, Tanya, have cycled around the world, and once rode from Calgary to Mexico with their three pre-teenaged sons. That's right, on bicycles and carrying all their gear.

Over 30 years, Rick and Tanya have travelled the world, first as a couple and then with their three boys as a family, on crazy adventures through regions both wonderous and terrifying – Mexico, Central America, Japan, Norway, Finland, New Zealand and many more – by their calculation they had racked up more than 100,000 kilometres on their touring bicycles. Through that, they have faced every form of adversity, from snow and days-long rain to flat tires, broken derailleurs, and bent wheels from crashes and breakdowns. By necessity, they had developed astonishing resilience and creative resourcefulness. It seemed that there was no mishap or challenge that Rick couldn't McGyver his way out of. Once, when the sidewall of a tire became shredded, Rick used a dollar bill to keep the tube intact until they could get to a bike shop. When a wheel broke from metal fatigue brought on by countless kilometres of travel, Rick found a way to put it back together with zip ties. When a guest's bicycle seat broke apart during a ride, Rick gave the rider his own seat and rode on a seatless bike for two days by standing on the pedals. And Tanya not only kept her partner on track, but she could also get camp organized and create a delicious meal out of whatever tired morsels of food we happened to still have with us.

Lisa and I, by comparison, were neophytes. Lisa is my wife, and a new bicycle touring enthusiast heading out on by-far her biggest challenge. Me, well, until recently I was a recreational cyclist who thought 50 kilometres on an unladen bike was a big day. An early 2020 two-week tour led by Rick in Argentina convinced me that I might be able to do a bit more than that. Even so, I was setting out not at all sure that I could even make it out of British Columbia, and yet willing to aim for an ambitious – some would say foolhardy – target. Throughout the tour, we would be joined by many others, as time permitted. Tanya joined us in Calgary and stayed until she had to return to Calgary from Montreal to run her day home in the fall. Andrew Hawes, who discovered our tour while surfing the internet, joined us in Princeton and stayed with us until he decided to strike out on his own in the middle of Saskatchewan. Allison Flach, a core member of the ConnecTour team, joined us in Calgary and stayed until we reached Thunder Bay, when she had to return home to start a new job. There were many others who came and went: Jennifer Herring, Lynn Marshall, Jessica Burylo, Doug Reid, Andy Williamson, Richard Briggs, Ray Quan and Coleen Ponzini. We stay in touch with most, and some have become fast friends – brothers and sisters in arms, forever Krazy-Glued together by a lived experience that cannot be described, can only be felt.

A year-and-a-half of planning seemed to be finally coming to fruition. The U.S. Center for Disease Control had just announced people fully vaccinated against COVID-19 could stop wearing masks, and the initial pandemic panic was easing. A well-connected source in the B.C. government led us to believe that travel restrictions were about to be eased, and that getting to Victoria would be allowed. This could finally be our time.

Our plan was to drive to Kelowna, where my daughter, Kyrsten, and her family live. She would then drive us to Victoria, where we would start the tour within a couple of days. But, as with so many well-laid plans, the COVID-19 pandemic had other ideas.

Our hearts sank during our drive west as we turned on the radio in the car and learned that, instead of loosening the rules, the B.C. government was in fact doubling down.

Non-emergency travelers would not be allowed to cross B.C.'s five health boundaries, which meant that as we listened to the report near the resort town of Golden it dawned on us that we were already in violation of the tightened rules.

Lapsing into denial, we considered an outlaw run for Victoria, but that short-lived fantasy evaporated when we heard from friends that non-essential travelers were being turned away at the Tsawassen Ferry. Dipping our wheels into the Pacific Ocean would have to wait.

So we drove to Kelowna, grabbed a few cans of IPA, and pondered our next move.

2. GETTING READY

A YEAR-AND-A-HALF OF PANDEMIC PLANNING

All great adventures start with an idea. It's often an implausible idea, and yet someone pursues it out of sheer stubbornness. But where do ideas come from anyway? Committees don't make ideas. Barnstorming doesn't create ideas. No. Ideas come from letting go – of the self-limiting mechanisms we use to ensure we navigate through day-to-day life. Letting go of the defence mechanisms that keep us from doing things that may stretch us beyond reasonable limits. That prevent us from harming ourselves. That – you might argue – prevent us from living our lives to the fullest because we just have to pay the mortgage, get the kids to soccer and top up the RRSPs. “Tragedy I take straight,” says Cutter in the novel by Newton Thornburg. “It's the daily grind that gets me.”

Our great idea started with beer.

Rick, Tanya, Lisa and I became close friends after we toured northwest Argentina with Rick’s company OnaVelo in early 2020, just before the full force of the pandemic shut the world down.

Argentina became our gateway drug. Carrying loaded rear panniers, we cycled at a leisurely pace through the bucolic towns, expansive wine regions and arid mountains of the region. This slow-motion pace allowed us to fully take in the richness of the ever-evolving landscape, to wave and shout greetings at the curious passersby and to absorb the seductive environment that enveloped us like a never-ending hug. In just a few short days, we had touched the soul of the country. We fell in love with the intoxicating charms of slow travel. We called it travelling at the speed of life.

Doug and Lisa: Argentina ride was our gateway drug.

But we were unplugged during the Argentina trip, and didn't really understand how rapidly the COVID-19 pandemic was unfolding. It wasn't until we spent a few post-tour days discovering Buenos Aires that we heard about it on the news. By the time we got to the airport to return home, people were wearing masks. And a day after we safely touched down in Calgary, the first of the international travel bans had kicked in.

Like everyone, we were quickly becoming hostages in our own homes by a plague that scientists were only beginning to get their heads around.

We would occasionally meet at Two House Brew in west Calgary. We often talked about the impact of COVID, on our friends, neighbours, family and co-workers. It had become a truly strange inflection point in 21st century history; a moment that made us fearful to shake a friend's hand, to brush close to strangers at the grocery store, and forced us to stand in half-hour lineups at the home renovation store and organize online social events through Zoom. Genuine face-to-face human interaction was on indefinite hold.

But we also relived key moments from the joyful experience of cycling through the bucolic South American countryside and talked about the redemptive power of bicycle touring. Naturally, the talk drifted into what our next adventure would be.

"I've always wanted to ride across Canada," said Rick, a man who has been across the U.S., through Europe, New Zealand, Japan, Norway and parts of Asia and South America. I was mildly surprised that in his three decades of riding, Canada had never made the cut.

"So have I," came a voice from a place inside of me that I barely recognized.

Lisa's head snapped my way, her eyes ablaze with both surprise and incredulity. "You've never told me that," she said, and I realized she was absolutely right. She later told me that after the initial shock, her internal voice said, "Yeah, like that'll ever happen."

What made me – a boring office-job guy who spent most of his pre-retirement years facing down a computer – blurt that out? Was it beer talk? (A bit.) Or was there some deeper craving that bubbled to the surface? I've always been the "solid" guy, the person who is willing to set aside my dreams in consideration of the people around me. Anyone who has raised kids on a tight budget will know exactly what I'm talking about. Over the years, there are many personal ambitions that I have not expressed because I dismissed them as, if not impossible, certainly well beyond practical. I'm also by nature very conservative in my commitments. I think that might have its roots in being raised by parents who experienced the Great Depression and spent the rest of their lives being very cautious with their money, and consequently with their indulgences.

But dreams never fully go away. In fact, as you age, a sense of urgency emerges with the realization that the clock never stops ticking. There are only so many tomorrows, and procrastination will eventually creep up and bite you in the ass. If you want to travel, it is much better to do so while you can still walk a dozen kilometres, eat and drink too much that evening, and then get up and do it again the next day. Recently, a good friend of mine died in a skiing accident right before my eyes. Other friends have died of COVID, and still others have been felled by cancer. When it chooses to be cruel, fate knows no friends and takes no prisoners.

But, almost miraculously, I found that you don't have to force your dreams to come back. You just have to believe that achieving them will be possible. Gradually, they bubble to the surface, at first so subtly you don't even notice. Stepping away from work helps immensely. After more than four decades of working first in newspapers and then communications, I finally accepted that it was OK to take a little "me" time – to explore the world with my beloved partner, jump out of a plane, ski the most extreme double-black run, walk up that mountain and hug a grizzly. (OK, just kidding about that last one.)

So, before I had time to ponder the implications, I was in. And, to my surprise, so was Lisa. We were going to join with Rick and Tanya and our mutual friend Allison Flach to ride our bicycles across Canada.

But why? Certainly, the adventure itself was reason enough. We thought of all the incredible sights and smells and sounds of this sprawling country that we would absorb, about the human encounters and about the test we would put our bodies to. At the time, I was 68 years old, and I was thinking of myself as someone on the downward slope of life. Could someone my age with no history of long-distance touring even contemplate such a journey? It didn't take long to discover that I was selling myself short. People much older than I have taken on much greater challenges and succeeded. But the group wanted more than just the adventure and physical challenge. We wanted this trip to somehow reflect the context of the time – the horrible pandemic that had shattered lives, broken communities and made us all prisoners in our own homes. So, over several more beers, we began to put shape to a sense of mission. Our ride would be about reconnecting with people, rebuilding a sense of community and restoring some of the bonds that hold this improbable nation together. It would not be about how many kilometres or how much elevation was gained in a day. It would not be about our average speed or what our aching joints might tell us. In fact, it wouldn't really be about us at all. It would be about the people we discovered, and about how they go about their lives can tell us about each other. It would be a tour of connections, which eventually led us to our group's name: ConnecTour.

I suppose you could just hop on a bicycle and head out across the country. Many have tried, and some of them even make it. But – thank God for our veteran tourer – Rick showed us a better way. The right way to set out on a months-long adventure is to train, secure the right gear, plan the meals, plot the route, look for financial support, seek out like-minded riders and pick the right time to go. It was late winter of 2020 when we agreed on doing the tour, and initially we thought it could happen over the summer. But as the COVID-19 pandemic evolved, it became clear group travel that year would be unrealistic. Provinces had closed their borders, and the fear of infecting, or being infected by, others was palpable. Surely, we thought with what later proved to be too much optimism, things will be better in 2021.

In the meantime, we created a website, set up a fundraising account, started talking to potential sponsors and searched for the right gear.

We quickly learned from would-be sponsors that there is no line that links abstract concepts, like reconnecting Canadians, to cash. We could ride to raise funds for cancer research, or to support a cause that fit with a corporate brand, or to promote Race Face, Surly, Arkel or some other product, but if we weren't willing to shill we were on own.

Eventually, we accepted that making the compromises needed

to secure such sponsorships just wouldn't fit with our vision of the ride. Even organizations we thought might make natural allies – like the Trans Canada Trail association – loved our idea but couldn't find any cash to help make it happen. Since we planned to avoid busy highways as much as possible, about one-third of our planned route would involve portions of the TCT. What a great way to tell Canadians about this amazing project, we argued. Ultimately, it was fortunate no funding came our way because it might have dampened our willingness to speak the truth about this underfunded, ungoverned and deeply flawed network of pathways. In the coming pages, you'll learn a bit more about why we feel this way.

There are many critical elements to a successful ride, and they include a willing mindset, a base level of fitness, adequate hydration, proper nutrition, all-weather camping gear, a good but compact set of tools and spare parts, and the resourcefulness to deal with almost daily unexpected turns of events. Oh, and did I mention a healthy measure of luck? One of the most critical elements is choosing the right bicycle.

There are many fine touring bikes on the market these days. Some favourites include the Kona Sutra, Surly Disc Trucker and Trek 520, although there are perhaps a dozen other models on recommended lists. On the road, we saw riders on an endless variety of mounts, and in some cases we wondered how they were able to get as far as they had. Our ride was to be "unsupported", which meant there was no van trailing behind us carrying our heavy gear. Everything we would need was mounted on our bikes: clothes, tents, stoves, pots and pans and whatever little creature comforts we could add, all while trying to keep the weight to a sustainable level. There's a sweet spot between what you need (it turns out, very little) and what you can carry over long distances. As your body gains strength, it can carry more weight, but there is a practical limit. For example, Andrew, a fit ex-military guy and first-time bike tourer, showed up in Princeton on his first day with what must have been 40 kilograms of gear. After one exhausting day of riding, he quickly began to unload the army boots, rappelling rope, tarps, insulated Thermos and other gear that was killing him.

In the middle of the pandemic, bicycles had suddenly become scarce – especially specialized single-purpose touring bikes. But Rick still had connections to a bicycle charity that he used to run in Calgary, and he was able to secure two surplus Surly Long Haul Truckers for Lisa and me at a reasonable price. Precursor to the current Disc Trucker, these Surlys have long been a favourite with cycling tourists.

The heavy-but-strong chromoly steel frames were next to unbreakable (and even then could be brazed back together), had pre-drilled fittings to attach racks to, heavy duty bearings meant to last for years, wheels with extra spokes that could bear heavy weight over long distances, fat, gravel-friendly tires, low gearing for climbing mountains . . . and even a place to attach spare wheel spokes – because, well, shit happens.

These were used bikes, though, and Rick was not about to let us set out on a 9,000-kilometre ride without giving them a thorough tune-up. In one very long day in Rick's bike-stuffed downtown Calgary garage, Lisa and I got a crash course in making a used bicycle virtually new. We replaced tires and tubes, chains, brakes and cables, shifter cables, the rear derailleur sprocket, bar tape and added fenders – almost everything that could wear out was switched out for something new. By the end of the day, we had not only learned a lot about bicycle mechanics, but we were also confident these rigs were fit to carry us as far as we were willing to go.

As it turned out, the only flat tire the two of us had was on my bike just a two-day ride outside of St. John's, NL (thanks to some ever-present roadside debris). And the only mechanical failure was a shattered bearing in the bottom bracket on my Surly in Repentigny, Quebec – a mishap that, by the sheer luck of being close to a bicycle shop, set us back about an hour.

EQUIPMENT

Hauling every gram of your gear with you sharpens the mind. You focus on what you truly need and jettison the rest. This is what we found we (mostly) had to have:

Camping Gear

- A quality wind-resistant, waterproof yet lightweight backpacking tent.
- Backpacking sleeping bags, just warm enough to help get you through nights as cold as 0C.
- Lightweight ground sheet.
- Lightweight tarp, such as a Sea to Summit Escapist

- Ultra-light compact camping chairs.
- Rechargable dome light

Rick's packing video: https://youtu.be/99-uq_gg-NE

Cooking & Eating

- Compact cutlery, and a washable plate, bowl and cup
- Compact back-packing style pots and pans
- Matches/lighter
- A backpacking stove, especially one that runs on a variety of fuels, including unleaded gasoline. (This came in handy in a number of remote locations.) Examples include the Primus OmniFuel or MSR WhisperLite.

Recipes

Cooking on the road is entirely dependent on your proximity to stores. Where no stores are nearby, our resident cooks became highly inventive. We did not carry any freeze-dried foods with us, choosing instead to cook fresh with whatever ingredients we had at our disposal. A collection of some of our favourite recipes appears at the end of this book. If anything, they prove you can almost always add a little style to your diet.

Clothing

- Two sets of cycling clothes, underwear, socks (one to wash while you wear the other)

- Cycling shoes, gloves and helmet. Warm gloves for cold mornings.
- End-of-day clothes, including a warm sweatshirt, shorts, and long pants
- Shoes, such as low-cut hikers, and a set of flip-flops for the shower.
- A lightweight down-filled jacket
- Swimsuit, for those steamy days when you're cycling by lakes
- Rain gear – especially a good rain jacket. We often did not wear rain pants because our legs would sweat in them. And our experiment with waterproof shoe covers was a total failure. A better option is waterproof socks to be worn with your cycling shoes.

Menus

You mostly cook what you can get your hands on. In areas with denser populations, access to grocery stores was relatively easy. Yet there were many other areas in which grocery store access was limited or didn't exist at all. In those areas, finding a small variety store that had anything was welcome.

Even with these challenges, our team came up with some delicious recipes. A few of our favourites appear at the end of this book.

THE CONNECTOUR CRUE

Rick, Tanya, Lisa, Allison and **I** were the ConnecTour core. But we invited others to join us for all or part of the journey. The team included:

Jennifer Herring: Then a student at the University of Calgary. This would be her first big ride.

Lynn Marshall: An accountant who lives in rural Alberta, near Diamond Valley, Alberta.

Jessica Burylo: An Edmonton-based public education outreach officer with Parks Canada.

Doug Reid: A retired General Motors employee living in Listowel, ON.

Andy Williamson: CEO of New Wave Exploration Inc., a geophysical consulting firm, and a session drummer living in Perth, ON.

Richard Guy Briggs: An open-source engineer and outspoken cycling advocate in Ottawa.

Ray Quan: A retired nuclear engineer living in Saint John, N.B.

Coleen Ponzini: A retired director of financial resources living in the Vancouver area.

And then, there was Drew.

Andrew Hawes is an ex-Canadian Forces soldier on a permanent pension and living with PTSD. By his own account, he has had a difficult life of big ups and even greater downs, including a full-scale personal crash that saw him drug-addled and living rough on the streets of Vancouver. At one point, he told us, even his beloved Surly Big Dummy cargo bike was seized by police because they didn't believe someone in his condition could actually afford to own it. By 2021, though, he was ready to crawl out of his hellish pit and start the long road to recovery. When he discovered on the ConnecTour website that we planned to bike across Canada, he decided that was a long enough road for him. He contacted Rick and asked to join the group.

Drew: an ex-soldier on a mission.

"He's a little different," Rick warned us. We would soon learn how different he was.

Everywhere Drew went, it seemed, drama would not be far behind. It started on the day he was to join us and needed to find a last-minute substitute driver to get him from Vancouver to our rendezvous point in Princeton, B.C., after his arranged driver bailed with the $400 Drew had given him. In the coming days, we realized that we were all part of Andrew's recovery team, listening to genuinely incredible stories about his days in the Armed Forces and after.

Drew told us that he was on full pension from the Armed Forces because an incident years ago that traumatized him and left him with deep emotional scars. He told us that he was stationed in Ontario at a time when two soldiers went rogue and threatened to go on a shooting spree. Andrew said his commanding officer told him to go their barracks, find them and shoot them before they could break out and harm others. Andrew said he got drunk and went there, and, not finding the two soldiers, ransacked the place. They had escaped. He said he later learned they had fled to the United States, and wounded someone there before they were captured.

As bizarre and implausible as this story is, I felt obliged to check it out. He is, after all, receiving a substantial pension, big enough, in fact, that it funds his activities. Unfortunately, I was not able to verify any of Drew's recounting of events. I did, however, find several war movies that deal with similar themes. For example, in the 2013 documentary called Kill Team, a group of American soldiers stationed in the Kandahar province of Afghanistan begin murdering local civilians under the influence of their commander Calvin Gibbs. Troubled by their behaviour, a soldier named Adam Winfield complains to his father in the U.S. It took the military months to respond, but eventually 11 soldiers were convicted of misconduct ranging from drug abuse to murder. Winfield said he was so terrified of his fellow soldiers he later took part in the murder of clergyman Mullah Allah Dad. Gibbs, the unit's commander, was sentenced to life in prison, and Winfield served just three years.

I wondered: Did our fellow cyclist Drew live the horrors he described to us? Or was his imagination fueled by the stories he had heard or seen? We didn't know then and perhaps will never know for certain. What we did know is that Drew had his own very personal reasons for being on this ride. And the rest of us were effectively part of his platoon. Each day, as we began our ride, he'd say, "I've got your back." And he did, bringing up the rear of the group and often riding his massive Big Dummy cargo bike into the middle of the lane to ensure traffic gave us a wide berth.

Like it or not, we had become our own little army of adventurers.

Our Ride Takes On New Purpose

Our team's job was to focus on the magical places and amazing Canadians we will meet. But Lisa and I were still looking for the "hook" – the reason, beyond the sheer adventure, to go on this ride. The answer came suddenly and unexpectedly as we were about to start our ride. Just two weeks before we were to start, it came to light that our son-in-law, Dax Grindler, was experiencing advanced liver failure. Doctors told Dax, a then-42-year-old athletic man, that the only way to save his life was to perform a liver transplant. They did not know how quickly it could, or must, happen, but said it depended a great deal on when the right organ could be found.

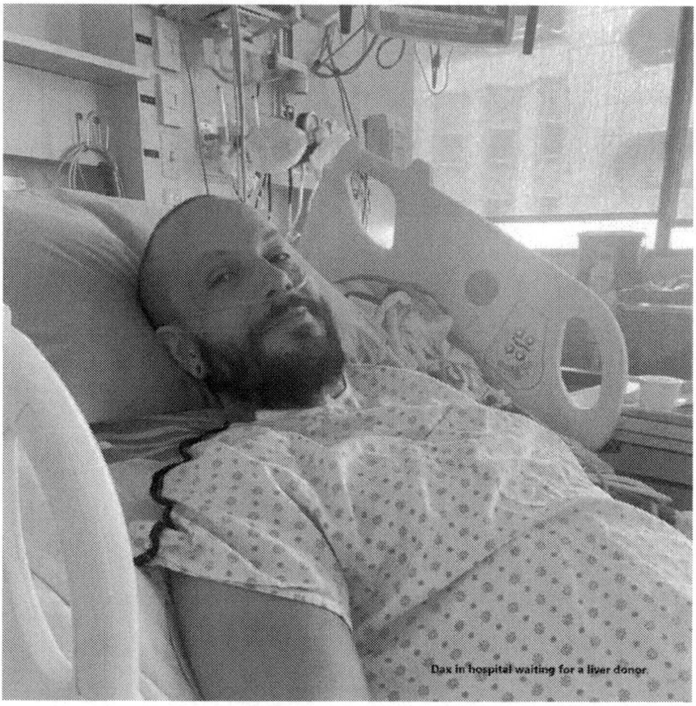

Dax in hospital waiting for a liver donor

You may have heard that many Canadians die each year waiting for an organ donation. The numbers are shocking. In 2019, the Canadian Institute for Health Information tells us, 1,789 kidneys were transplanted in Canada, accounting for the majority of single-organ transplants. Other organs transplanted included 610 livers, 212 hearts, 404 lungs and 68 pancreases. Tragically, though, that same year 250 Canadians died waiting for a donated organ and, at the end of 2019, 4,400 patients were waiting for a transplant. Yet, in most provinces only about one-third of people who could donate organs have registered to do so.

Dax has battled several serious medical challenges over the years, including ulcerative colitis, testicular cancer and now liver failure. He has Primary Sclerosing Cholangitis (PSC), a rare liver condition that afflicts around five per cent of people with ulcerative colitis. A liver transplant would give Dax and partner Lauren a shot at a full and happy life together; failure to find a suitable liver donation would amount to a death sentence.

This ride had become very personal for me and Lisa. This ride was now for Dax, and to raise awareness of the life-gift of organ donation.

3. PNR: BRITISH COLUMBIA

"I've lived in BC for fifteen years, and I've been saying this the whole time. It's like a mix of elitism and entitlement and general coldness maybe? . . . Once you get out of the lower mainland, the folks get way better."

"If you can live somewhere that beautiful and be an asshole I'd be surprised!"

From Reddit Thread r/britishcolumbia

MAY – A LITTLE HEAVEN, A LITTLE HELL

Tire pressure: check

Chain lube: check

Nuts and bolts tightened: check

Snack bars in the handlebar bag: check

Panniers stuffed and firmly affixed: check

Odometer set to 0: check

Heart rate elevated: check

This shit is finally getting real. Today is Day 1 and we are at the PNR – the point of no return. No excuses. No cold feet. No graceful off-ramp. Too much invested to back down now. PNR.

The Kettle Valley Rail Trail – a few kilometres southeast of Kelowna – is a spectacular and scenic bike route that winds through the Myra Valley Canyon. Part of the Trans Canada Trail (formerly Great Trail) system, this historic former railroad with its wooden rail trestles seemed a fitting place from which to launch our cross-Canada venture. There were four of us on this day: Rick, Lisa, Jennifer (who we quickly nicknamed Double-N Jenn) and me. Our plan was to ride the trail south to Penticton, then follow it west to Princeton where we would meet up with another member of our group. Then, we would set a tsetse fly-like path that would, with an equal measure of bull-headed determination and good luck, eventually deliver us in St. John's, NL. Rick had devoted countless hours to plotting out the route day-by-day, adjusting the distances travelled to accommodate elevation gain and our growing fitness as the trip unfolded. Our first day was to be a relatively leisurely 65-kilometre cruise down the gentle two-degree slope on the old railroad bed into Penticton, where we would crash at the home of an old high school buddy of mine.

Oh, the plan. If only.

We wound our way up the Myra Forest Service Road, unloaded the little red truck, hitched up our panniers, and felt the weight of the moment settled upon us. This was it. After a year-and-a-half of planning, daily hand-wringing over COVID-19, and countless logistical challenges, this would be our first small step on what us newbies in particular saw as an epic journey – one that would be full of uncertainties and adventure and that would test our physical limits in ways we could not yet imagine.

Right from the start, I doubted my ability to complete the trip. A couple of days before our ride's start, I had gone out with Rick and Jenn for a warmup ride outside of Kelowna. Though it wasn't a hard ride, when I pushed my way up some small hills, I felt a sudden onset of dizziness and vertigo. Near passing out, several times I had to get off my bike and wait for the sky to stop spinning. How, I wondered, could I ever ride across the country in a state like this?

That night, I researched the side-effects of some medication I was taking for a prostate condition – tamsulosin – and saw that dizziness and light-headedness were common. To hell with it, I told myself, I'm off the meds.

Even in the temperate world of central British Columbia, spring mornings were near freezing, forcing us to wear jackets and gloves. None of us thought or talked about the ultimate destination of St. John's, NL – it was too far to even contemplate. Instead, today's destination, Penticton, was top of mind. Waiting for us at Myra Canyon was Jim Barr, the "Doc Pow" social media founder and anchor of Seekers Media. Lisa had worked for several years as editor of the Seekers online publications, and Jim was there to help us launch in style. Because we weren't able to dip our wheels in the Pacific Ocean, he brought a can of Okanagan Springs 1516 lager which he poured into a frisbee for the symbolic dip. Then he ran with us as we shakily headed out on our heavily laden bikes.

The first eight kilometres of the ride was a stunning tour across the trestles, overlooking deep and wild valleys. I remember thinking, I could do this all the way across Canada. But our euphoria was short-lived. As we reached the end of the "tourist loop," the rail suddenly and drastically descended into an almost impassible construction zone. Work crews were repairing eroded sections of the trail, and had added in coarse, sharp stones about the size of fast balls. We hopped off our bikes, and gingerly walked them through the rubble.

What we found on the other side was even worse. The gravel trail, so perfect in the trestle area, had transformed into a series of deep potholes filled with muddy water – ripped apart by the ATVs that literally tear through these so-called multi-use trails.

As we walked our bikes through the most treacherous areas, our new cycle shoes became saturated, and we fell into the giddy laughter of people confronted with the absurd. Three of the four in the group at that point crashed in the next two hours.

Rick tried to ride through one puddle, hit a deep trough and narrowly avoided being thrown over the handlebars. Soon, there was a thunderstorm of F-bombs. It was mid-afternoon by the time we reached Chute Lake, just halfway to our planned first-day destination. Google Maps optimistically predicted the entire distance would take 3:11 on a bike, but it took us five hours to get just half that distance. We stopped at the lodge for beer and spotted a recreation site nearby where we could camp. "Fuck it," said Rick. Amen, we chimed in.

It dipped below freezing that first night at the Chute Lake Rec Site, but we didn't care. We had toughed it out through a disappointing Day 1 and put our butterflies to bed. The trail gradually improved as we rolled gently toward Penticton in the morning, feeling the warm sun speckled through the trees. By midday we reached town, where I planned to meet up with an old high school buddy, John Singleton, and his partner, Char. After a leisurely beer in a downtown park, we set out once again on the Kettle Valley pathway for an uphill climb north and west towards Summerland as we traced our way toward Princeton.

Once again, though, the trail would prove to be a wicked challenge. This time, as we climbed out of Penticton and fought our way up towards Summerland, our tires sank into the trail's loose sand, making every pedal stroke exhausting. It took us until late in the day to reach our off-grid camping spot near the tiny hamlet of Bankeir. My daughter Kyrsten and her family had driven from West Kelowna with their Wrangler and camped the night with us.

The next morning, we said goodbye to Kyrsten and Dave, and headed towards Princeton. As we slogged our way on the trail towards Princeton, we spotted a gravel road that ran roughly parallel and quickly realized that the best way to reach our destination that day would be to ditch the trail and head for the road. Lisa said it best as we climbed down an incline to the road: "Great fucking trail!"

It's hard not to be emotional after our first three days on the road. We had gone through what effectively felt like an unplanned boot camp. The group took a day to rest in Princeton, a quaint little on-again-off-again mining town of about 2,800 people.

When I was talking with Eleanor McMahon, the CEO of the Trans Canada Trail association in Ottawa, about getting some financial support, I described the trail as aspirational. The implied message is that, in its current state, the TCT is less than it aspires to be. I could tell from her reaction she didn't like the description, but it's true. There are portions of the trail, especially in Ontario, that are quite lovely and rideable. Yet, many of the sections of the trail we rode were, at best, suitable for an unladen mountain bike. For touring bikes, they were useless.

I asked Spencer Coyne, the humble hoser-mayor of Princeton about the trail the next day, after I chased him down to The Source store, where he was working checkout. This is the same Spencer Coyne who a year later would find himself in the whirlwind of media attention as the Similkameen and Tulameen rivers breeched their banks and washed away the time-standing-still stasis that makes these interior B.C. towns so irresistible. When I talked to Spencer, Princeton was just a sleepy town of mostly 2,800 retirees and frustrated teenagers. None of us could have known at that point the cruel twist of fate that lay ahead for this charming little interior-B.C. town. In November 2021, the town was inundated with floods – but on this day, that disaster was still in the future.

Spencer, a short, chubby and affable man, was sporting an ascot cap and untucked plaid short-sleeve shirt when I caught up with him. He told me he loves the KVR. But when I asked him why the town doesn't just ban ATVs and other off-road vehicles from tearing it up, he let out the uncomfortable chuckle of someone who realizes he has to explain the facts of life to a Big City Guy.

The short answer is that any politician who wants to keep his job doesn't tangle with the ATV set. Who gets to use the KVR is a huge bone of contention in the area.

Princeton Mayor Spencer Coyne

A previous council that had tried to ban ATVs from using the trail ended up getting tossed out on its ear in 2018, and that's when Spencer made the transition from irreverent newspaper columnist to head of the local government.

While he sympathized with our complaint, he favoured keeping the KVR multi-use: "It's been motorized since there was a train there," he said.

He blamed B.C.'s provincial government for not providing enough money to maintain the trail properly, and he said the lack of support fuels the conflict.

"It's always everybody fighting with each other," he says. "The bikers say the ATVs rip it up, and they (the ATV riders) blame the horses. It's unfortunate. I'm a big advocate for the KVR."

The TCT's McMahon explained that the federal group has no jurisdiction over the regional sections of the trail. The national body, in effect, channels funds that are raised to areas across the country where it feels it will best be spent. Clearly, the section outside of Princeton was not a priority.

Princeton has a bucolic campground right beside the river. It was there we were joined by Andrew Hawes, the fifth member of the group who had literally jumped through hoops to join us.
He was so joyful to be with us after months of planning, he was near tears. Andrew, a massive muscular hulk of a man, lives in a Canadian military pension because he suffers from PTSD as a result of some truly incredible experiences he claims to have gone through. He would, through sheer force of his personality, end up heavily shaping the first half of our ride. By every measure, he was a person of extremes – extreme strength, extreme equipment, over-the-top personality, extreme loyalty to his fellow riders and an irresistible impulse to interject and dominate conversations.

Drew with his overloaded cargo bike.

June – Settling Into A (Sweaty) Groove

Hot and starting to feel fatigued after a vigorous three-hour run from Penticton on our way to Keremeos, the five of us were looking for one of B.C.'s famous rec sites to have a picnic as we approached Keremeos on Highway 3. As much as we could, we stayed off highways on our trip, and the day started on Old Hedley Road until we were forced to jump back onto the highway. Although there had been plenty of treed rec sites on Old Hedley, none, it seems, existed on the main road.

So, as the searing 35-plus degree heat began to wear us down, we sought refuge at an RV park picturesquely situated on the Similkameen River, still churning furiously with the spring runoff.

As we pulled into the Riverside RV Park, we saw a park-like setting with shady trees and a welcoming grassy area. A bearded man wearing a cowboy hat pulled up in a tired old black Frontier pickup to see what we were up to. A dog beside him on the front seat peered out, apparently looking for a treat.

"Do you think it's OK if we have our lunch here?" one of us asked.

"I don't know," came the reply as he looked at us quizzically. "I just live here."

We took a chance and headed to a picnic table down by the riverside. Not 10 minutes in, we saw the same man walking towards us with a large jug of water in one hand and a bag of ice in the other. He introduced himself as Ian, and his dog Brewskie.

"Sorry about the way I reacted back there," he said, as Brewskie sniffed our snacks. "I should have invited you over to my place."

Just five days into our journey, it was our first glimpse into the nature of the common people of Canada. This would be just the first in dozens of unexpected encounters with kind and caring Canadians as we worked our way across the country. They were everywhere: From the park resident who insisted on taking our picture for the local TV station to Chris, the campground manager at 1877 Grist Mill just outside of Keremeos, who told us to, "Just set up. We'll settle up in the morning," to the truck driver who threw us a can of sunscreen because it was the only thing he had to offer us at the moment. Time and again, we encountered curiosity, friendliness and helpfulness on a scale we didn't expect and that left us feeling humbled and warm. It is a big country; over the coming months we could come to appreciate just how big it is. And yet, despite the geography that separates us, this massive and baffling country retains a sense of community and communality that keeps this 150-year-old grand social experiment alive.

Day 1 took its toll on Drew.

Lisa describes our next day:

Rolling into the Grist Mill Campground at Keremeos on a blistering

30-plus day after a 76-kilometre day on our bikes, we were ready to find a place to cool down, camp for the night and rest with a light dinner and a few cold ones.

As we have quickly learned on this trip, the serendipity soon begins.

The campground just on the edge of town in Keremeos is as adorable as campgrounds go, set alongside a fast-moving river amid the trees, a beautiful perennial garden and an historic grist mill onsite. Chris Mathieson, the facility manager, greeted us and asked what we were doing loaded down with all that gear. We told him about the vision behind ConnecTour.

Across our campsite sat a tall, gangly young man named Scott. We learned he'd been homeless for 10 years and was trying to find some sense of normalcy after a life of hardship, drug addiction and other obstacles life had thrown at him. He wore his heart on the sleeve of what he called his "wizard" jacket. He and Chris, the manager, had worked out a deal in which Scott would work in the campground to pay for his site. Scott ambled over, and as he talked with us, he revealed his war stories from being homeless and addicted on the streets of East Vancouver.

Scott's stories touched a nerve with Andrew, our former military man. After leaving the military, Andrew, we had learned, spent time on the streets of Vancouver as a drug addict. He had been right on life's edge, as had Scott. Yet Andrew was further down the long, hard path to recovery than Scott was, and he knew he could be of help.

Scott had next to nothing to his name, save his meagre camping gear and his "rock fridge" on the bank of the river to keep his food cool. Andrew was ready to start shedding the excessive gear he had acquired for his first-ever bike-packing tour. We marvelled how he made it through his first day under a searing sun. It quickly became apparent Andrew would need to unload a hefty amount of gear if he wanted to enjoy (and survive) the first of many hilly terrains to come on our 110-day journey. We were to begin our next multi-climb leg into Osoyoos – never mind the prediction of a scorching 38 C day.

Over a beverage at the picnic table, it was decided that Andrew could hand off his multiple t-shirts, heavy hiking boots, a massive tarp, a super-long and heavy laundry line, a headlamp and a classic Stanley mug – among the ultimately 30 pounds-plus of gear to Scott.

The handoff began, as Andrew began making the hard decisions of what gear to give up so that he could ride joyfully.

"It reminded me that it's better to give than to receive," said Andrew. "It felt good. His life on the streets taught him how to use all these things."

"Scott was like 'wow,'" said Andrew. In particular, he appreciated the tarp for sun protection, which went up immediately.

As we packed up early the next morning, we had no idea what Scott was thinking as he watched us go. What I was thinking is something about the delightful lightness of being. Travelling on a bike – effectively our mobile home for the summer – and giving and receiving serendipitous gifts.

It was now the second day of June. The next morning, we set out on another blistering hot day to ride the 48 kilometres to Osooyos. We ambled along the relatively quiet Highway 3, which traces the winding Similkameen River, but had to finish the day with a gruelling grind up Mount Richter. The payoff was a long, speedy float downhill into Osooyos. There we were met by Don Urquhart, a reporter for the South Okanagan Times Chronicle newspaper. He had chosen to settle into small town journalism after travelling the world. Here's what he wrote:

Coast-To-Coast Cyclists Make Pit Stop In Osoyoos

Posted by Times-Chronicle | Jun 11, 2021

By Don Urquhart

Huddling in the shade of Veterans Memorial Park on a day the mercury was tipping 38 celsius, the cyclists behind the cross-Canada

ConnecTour looked up at the ribbon of road wending its way up and over Anarchist Mountain.

Their faces flushed from the sun and weary from the ride from Keremeos, they surveyed the next day's challenge. "That's two hours and four litres of water!" Doug Firby, one of the core team of the cycling adventure, laughed wryly about the next day's uphill ride.

The group of cycling adventurers led by long-time cycle tour leader Rick McFerrin, who has a lifetime of cycle touring all over the globe, aimed to travel more than 8,000 km from Victoria, B.C. to St. Johns, Newfoundland in a bid to "reconnect, restore and rebuild" a sense of community that has been deeply wounded in the COVID-19 pandemic.

The group highlights the fact the pandemic has left Canadians reeling from this once-in-a-lifetime event, causing many to question assumptions "about what community is and what we want from ourselves and our society."

A year-and-half in the planning, the tour's impetus was simply this: "We started talking about how hard it's been on everyone in the country. It's really affected how we interact with each other as neighbours, lots of good things but people are stressed out and there is a sense of disconnectedness," Firby said.

"So we thought let's do a ride that will meet people in small communities, like this one, and talk to them about what's important to them and really get a sense of where we are as a nation as we come out of this pandemic."

It will in essence provide a snapshot of where we are as a country right now, not through the eyes of politicians or health authorities, but rather through the eyes of regular people. Along the way, the group will be joined here-and-there by people riding for just an hour or two, to weeks.

One of the challenges, he adds, is that 15 months ago when they were planning this, they thought things might be under control at this point. And while things are looking brighter, Canada is clearly not out of the woods yet.

With strict adherence to COVID-19 protocols, including daily temperature checks, the group had to abandon its original plan to begin in Victoria because of regional travel restrictions.

"One of the things we know is that it's possible we will get to a provincial border and they'll say 'it's closed' and that will be the end of the tour," Firby said. The one thing they do have on their side is time.

As Firby's partner Lisa Monforton noted, Manitoba is having difficulty now, "but we're not going to be there until the beginning of August and that's still a full two months away. A lot can change in that time."

Last Wednesday they arrived in Osoyoos, their journey having brought them from Keremeos and before that Princeton,

The ride down the famous KVR Trail brought much consternation due to the poor quality of the trail, which is part of Canada's Great Trail network.

While they try as much as possible to stay off the main highways, they often have no choice. Taking the old Hedley Road, for instance, it eventually petered out forcing them onto the Crowsnest Highway.

"I've driven up and down No. 3 more times than I can count," said Firby, "but when you go by that landscape on a bicycle and you're going 10 or 15 km/h you see things you've never noticed before."

Averaging around 75 km a day, they've had days as low as only 35 km, like on poorly maintained sections of the KVR Trail. The prairies are the shining light at the end of the literal and figurative tunnels, where seemingly endless flat land will enable 100 to 120 km a day.

Although only in the very early stages of a journey that will theoretically end in early October, already the group has been inspired by the kindness and conversations of people they've met along the way.

From Ian who brought out a big pitcher of water and another of ice as the group rested on the hot trek from Princeton to Keremeos, or the gifting of excess equipment by cyclist Andrew Hawes to a young guy named Scott who is living minimally in a campsite, having been homeless for 10 years and is now struggling towards a new life free of drug addiction.

The group also had a frank conversation about the poor state of the KVR Trail with Princeton Mayor Spencer Coyne.

"That's the kind of thing we're discovering already on this ride. That people are excited to see us doing this little trip, I think some of them get what we're all about and they want to do little things that will support us along the way," Firby added.

One of the biggest challenges the group faces is not the physical obstacles, although that's nothing to sniff at, it's the mental aspect.

"There will be days when you face a strong headwind or climbing up a very long hill and you actually have the physical stamina to do it, but it's a bit of a psychological issue," Firby said.

"On the plus side we are really drawing a lot of inspiration from people that we are meeting along the way," he added. This includes people honking, waving, and shouting out encouragement out their

car windows.

"I'm used to drivers yelling at me for being on the road," said another member of the group, Jennifer Herring. "But this one guy rolls down his window and yells 'good for you!' and another, 'you're doing great!'."

Along the way, the group is holding roughly 13 or 14 events typically revolving around cycling education and promotion such as bike tuning and rallies, with the next one scheduled for Calgary.

Putting the tour in context McFerrin urges Canadian's to truly appreciate and experience the country when of course it's safe to do so.

"I've had great experiences abroad, and now I'm really looking forward to having those experiences right here at home. I think it speaks a lot to the idea that we often think we've got to go to Europe or Southeast Asia to have those experiences, but you know what, let's look at what we have here in this great big country and explore it and share those stories.

"Why not just do it here, by car, by bike, by whatever, and really celebrate this country and acknowledge that we live in a great place."

As we finished our interview with Don, we turned our thoughts to where we might stay that night. Part of the bargain you make in unsupported bike touring is the uncertainty of where you will stay. With more than 100 days of travel, nightly hotel stays were way beyond our budget and, as it turns out, often way off our route.

Instead, for much of our trip, we either rough-camped or turned to an organization called Warmshowers for accommodations. It's a volunteer group, in which people who are friendly to cyclists will either let them camp in their backyard or loan a spare bed or two for the night.

It was a great way to connect with like-minded adventures, but, as luck would have it, no one in Osoyoos was listed as a Warmshowers host. After striking out with a couple of casual acquaintances, we found a beautiful beach-side campsite at the NK'MIP Nation, where the warm lake waters beckoned us to wash off the day's sweat. The only downer was the $100 with tax it cost to set up four tents on two sites. It was the most we paid to camp anywhere on the trip. I guess you could consider it a little guilt money for two centuries of colonial rule.

As we learned in the morning, our leader, Rick, delivers good news – and bad – only when he thinks people can handle it. He knows that some facts simply would not be accepted in the early going. Like this one: There are no hills.

Rick says there are no hills, only dips. For a long time, I simply got pissed off at him and refused to accept what he was saying. Eventually, though, his message about the hills began to make sense to me.

There are no hills. There is only riding. Some days of riding are slower than others. Our journey today to Midway would be one of them.

I've driven east out of Osoyoos before and probably noted that the drive involved a lot of hill-climbing. Cycling on a loaded bike, however, forever changed the way I think about that road. It is an experience that taxed our still-developing muscles to the limit and put our willpower to the first serious test.

The 870-metre vertical gain up Anarchist Mountain over about 20 kilometres of relentless climbing in mid-30s degree heat was the first of many demanding climbs we would encounter on the road to St. John's, and we were determined not to concede defeat so early in the game.

For those who haven't done this on a bicycle, those numbers probably won't mean a lot. Let me help you picture it – imagine doing a spin class at the gym, and the instructor is yelling at you to go harder and harder. Then, imagine that instead of a five-minute burst followed by a cool-down, you do that extreme exertion for four, five or six hours.

Rick, annoyingly, sloughed the climb off – "It's just a little dip" – although he convinced us to start the ride in the cool at 7 a.m. and was careful to ensure we packed enough water to stay hydrated.

Big hills? There's a way to do this. In fact, there's only one way to do this. You must be well-rested. It helps to have a huge breakfast and pack lots of energy bars to go with all that water. Then, you click the bike down to "granny gear" – the one that is just slightly faster than walking – put your head down and don't look more than 100 metres up the road. You have a job to do. It's going to take most of the day. Don't dwell on it. If ever there's a time to be the steady tortoise, this is it.

By the time we broke for lunch at around 2 p.m., we had made great progress, but still had kilometres to go. Eventually, we cracked the summit, only to discover after a few kilometres of relatively easy riding that we had another 100-metre climb. By then, fatigue and heat exhaustion were taking their toll and our water supply was running dangerously low.

But we made it – reaching another summit which, somewhat anticlimactically, just gently rolls into a downhill slope. After a joyous downhill cruise, we rolled into Midway for a cold smoothie and then made camp at the municipal Riverside Campground. There – as in almost every place we stopped – the people who greeted us almost universally said, "You're riding to where?"

St. John's, NL. Most days, the ultimate destination seemed too preposterous to even contemplate.

Not surprisingly, this was not one of our longest rides. When we rolled into the little hamlet of Midway another 30 k down the road, we were happy to find a campsite with showers at Riverside Park. There, we entertained incredulous trailer-campers with tales of our ambition. Though they were polite, I wondered how many of them believed we would actually make it to St. John's.

Talking to sponsors, I learned that one of the reasons many of them are so reluctant to come on board anymore is because of past experience. Countless cyclists have made pitches for either financial support or gear donations each year on the promise of being sea-to-sea brand ambassadors. But many never make it. Some quit just a few days or weeks in.

What made us different? In the early days, pride kept us going through some of the tougher days. It's also leadership, riding with someone who had prevailed through much greater adversity than we would face on this trip. And, as time went on, we were also lifted by the growing collegiality in our amorphous group, as we shared the excitement of exploring the country.

Then, there comes a moment when your body stops hurting. And when, what at first might seem like an insurmountable challenge morphs into just another step along the path. You get addicted to the routine, the pleasure of striking out each morning for an energetic 20-kilometre sprint before the first snack-stop of the day; the leisurely lunch stops in some grassy church yard; the magic way in which 70 kilometres-to-go turns into 50 and then 20, and suddenly you're there.

Ultimately, though, I think what drove me more than anything was the immeasurable pleasure of meeting the most unlikely people in the most unlikely places, getting to know a bit about them, and sharing our thoughts about what really matters to us. Not about the headlines of the day, but the headlines of our lives.

The next day, as I made my way for a morning shower at the park, I met an amiable man named Ken Gasman, who told me he had ridden his motorcycle around the world. Fascinated, I probed his background and learned he had worked in explosives for a time. "That job was a blast," he deadpanned, as though he hadn't used the pun 1,000 times before. Now, he's a realtor, which, to me, is a career that seemed to explain his gift for gab.

Refreshed and feeling pretty damn good about our first big accomplishment, we left early the following morning on the road to Greenwood.

Like Princeton, only hipper, Greenwood is truly one of the interior B.C. towns that are locked in time. It is a place where conscientious objectors from the U.S. traveled to evade the draft in the late 1960s and early '70s. It is a place where old frame buildings fill Main Street, looking not much different than they must have 50 or even 100 years ago. It is a place where massive slag heaps remain from a smelting operation that shut down decades ago.

And it is where we met Bruce and Katie Jensen at the Deadwood

Cafe. These aging hippies looked as though they had time-traveled forward five decades. Bruce was dressed in a bowtie and top hat.

Bruce and Katie Jensen: rockin' the cafe.

On the stereo, Blue Cheer was playing the psychedelic version of Summertime Blues. While Katie served up cups of coffee and snacks, Bruce told us there is a TV crew in town for the program Canadian Paranormal doing a segment on the ghosts at city hall. In this town full of spirit, it is easy to believe it is also full of spirits.

Greenwood has had its brushes with fame. It has been used as a set in movies. A 2019 novel by Michael Christie, claimed the town was named after the fictional logging magnate of Everett Greenwood. It got its start way back in 1886, when a prospector staked several copper core mining claims. By 1895, merchant Robert Wood erected a log store and named the region Greenwood and within a year there were three hotels, a general store, a livery stable, two assay offices, a mining broker, an opera house, and a dozen other establishments. By the turn of the century, 3,000 people lived there and the BC Copper Company began operating a smelter. Yet, within 10 years, people began to leave town as the boom went bust. By the end of the First World War in 1918, the copper market was dead, and the smelter in Greenwood was shut down. Today, it has a population of just over 700 people, and a massive slag heap as an ugly reminder of its long-dead heyday as a mining Mecca.

We carried on toward Grand Forks, another quiet town of 4,000 mostly retirees. We met up with Rick's friend Wayne at the top of the Eholt Summit. A retired RCMP officer who is reluctant to even acknowledge his old career, Wayne has been on two or three trips in Argentina with Rick. He's in his 70s, but even as he complained about the pace of riding he left the rest of us in his dust.

By early afternoon, we rolled into Grand Forks and headed for a downtown lunch shop called the Wooden Spoon. There we ran into Helen and Ed from Victoria. Hearing about our project, Helen exclaimed, "You guys are fantastic."

Delivered at the right moment, a few words can have a powerful impact. It feels like some higher power is sending us little bits of encouragement, just when we're feeling fatigued or discouraged.

We had arranged to meet the editor of the Grand Forks Gazette at the Wooden Spoon.

The young journalist, Laurie Tritschler, initially seemed like a surly and suspicious guy. He wondered out loud why we're on the road. Are we some of those anti-vaxxers? Don't we know we're in a pandemic? We assured him we were taking strict precautions, including masking, daily temperature checks and requiring participants to be up to date on their vaccinations.

Only then did he start to relax and open up about the impoverished life of small-town journalists. He was depressed and confessed he had little hope for the future of journalism. And yet as we told our story, he became animated and engaged. Here's what he wrote:

B.C. group to cycle across Canada to promote community spirit amid pandemic gloom

Calling themselves 'ConnecTour,' the group said they hope to reach the East Coast by the fall

LAURIE TRITSCHLER Jun. 7, 2021

A group of friends is cycling across Canada to promote a sense of community in the wake of the COVID-19 pandemic.

Having launched their 8,000-kilometre "Connectour" from Kelowna on May 28, The Gazette caught up with the riders during a pit stop in Grand Forks Friday, June 4.

"People are feeling disconnected right now," spokesperson Doug Firby explained.

"So, we thought, 'let's find people on the road and see if we can't rekindle some community.'"

The group hopes to reach St. John's, N.L. by October, but Firby granted that the tour might have to clear some logistical hurdles along the way.

"The big wildcard for us is what's happening with inter-provincial COVID-restrictions," he said.

"We're confident that as we roll east, people will have had their vaccinations and provincial borders will open before us — kind of like waves on the ocean."

Firby said the group maintains strict COVID-19 safety protocols, starting with daily self-checks for viral symptoms. All participants have to show a negative COVID-19 test result dated within 72 hours of joining the ride.

The riders have designated grocery shoppers to minimize contact with people outside the team, he continued.

Firby and his wife Lisa Monforton added that they also hope to spread awareness of the need for organ donors. Their 42-year-old son-in-law, recently diagnosed with liver disease, needs a transplant, they said.

The riders said they hoped people would track their progress through their website at connectour.ca.

For information about how to become an organ donor, contact BC Transplant's website at transplant.bc.ca.

Wayne invited us to set up camp in his backyard. Soon, an ebullient neighbour called John came over towing a gas grill and an electric guitar. He told us he's an EMS worker but he's also someone who is battling an addiction to alcohol. As he started playing old rock 'n roll tunes, I saw him slip his hand into his shirt and pull out a mickey. The music carried on into the evening and John convinced one of our crew to hit the local pub. Looking at Rick's haggard face the next morning, the rest of us were glad we took a pass.

Wayne rode with us for a few kilometres the next morning as we set out for the climb that would take us to Nancy Green Provincial Park. Along the way, at Christina Lake, a local cyclist joined in with the group. Hearing about our mission, he told us about Arvin Loewen, the Winnipeg-based cyclist who crossed Canada in 13 days and six hours (only to be beaten by Bruckner, the cyclist from Inuvik). Yet, we soon discovered that our tagalong rider had his own reasons for chatting us up. Befriending Jenn, he pulled out a copy of The Way, the Truth, and the Life, from the Gideons and urged her to give it a read. Then he headed back to Christina Lake – one guesses, in search of his next conquest. We soon found out that we could use someone to show us the way.

After a quick coffee at the Christina Lake visitor's centre, we set out on our biggest climb to date – 1,100 metres of altitude gain to Nancy Green Provincial Park. But instead of searing heat, our latest challenge was finger-numbing cold that made the last few kilometres to the park a harrowing experience.

Folks who live in the interior of B.C. like to joke that this month is "Juneuary." One day, it can be scorching hot, and the next day, it can be deathly cold. Knowing you are at the mercy of the weather can be a pretty abstract concept until you live it up close and personal in the valleys and mountains of this fickle province.

As we clawed our way up the steady grade, the clear day started to cloud over. When it started to sprinkle, Lisa and I – who were a bit behind the others – threw our rain jackets over our T-shirts. It turned out to be a dangerous miscalculation.

Within 15 minutes, the mountain sprinkle settled into a steady rain, punctuated by plummeting temperatures – and we had only our light rain jackets to protect us. We could see no sheltered place to suit up in full rain gear, so we decided to continue with what we had on. Again, a foolish mistake.

As we broke the summit and started the downhill run to the park, our hands were so cold we could barely grasp our brake levers. Unable to slow her bike, Lisa decided to walk but I could feel the hypothermia crimping every motion as it sunk ever deeper into our hands, feet, legs and eventually torsos.

Desperate for any place to find refuge, I spotted a concrete outhouse ahead. We parked our bikes outside and stood in the shelter trying to warm up our hands enough so that we could suit up in full rain gear. We must've been there for 20 minutes or more when a silver Porsche rolled up and an impatient driver came up to the outhouse and asked us if we were done in there. We laughed and yielded the outhouse, only to return to its shelter so we could finish suiting up.

The rest of the ride to the provincial park couldn't have been more than five kilometres, but it seemed to take an eternity to get there. Although we got our hands working, we were still deeply chilled as we hobbled our way along the busy highway. Transport trucks, cars and 4x4s roared by us, some so close we were showered in road spray and rocked by the wind gusts. It felt like piling insult onto injury.

I thought to myself, "If only some of those drivers could see the world from the seat of a bicycle right now." But we got there and found Rick anxiously waiting by the side of the road. We were the better part of an hour behind the group, and our fellow riders were imagining we had fallen prey to disaster. Turns out, we were saving disaster for later. As were rolled into the park, a couple in a Subaru who had spotted us on the road pulled up to make sure Lisa and I weren't in serious trouble.

We found shelter under the awning of an old boarded-up

cookhouse. A woman with a pronounced German accent approached us from her RV. Annie had been watching the chilled group roll into the park and concluded we needed a helping hand. Grabbing a screwdriver, she undid the screws holding the cookhouse door closed, so we could go in and start a fire to warm up. The floor was scattered with dead mice and their droppings, but we valued the warmth from that old stove a lot more than we cared about the state of the building. Bill and Elaine, who were camping in their RV a few spots away, chopped some wood for us and gave us enough to keep the fire going all evening. Rick, meanwhile, had set up the campsite, lit a campfire and had hot tea ready. As the day's rain gave way to a warm bath of late afternoon sun, we were able to cook an evening meal of quesadillas and start to dry out our soaked cycling shoes by the campfire.

Annie: A welcome arrival with a screwdriver.

The next morning was sunny and beautiful as we headed to Trail. Although it is set in the heart of what the government calls "Super, Natural British Columbia," Trail cannot be described as a pretty town. Its core is occupied by a rusty metal refinery that belches smoke into the pristine air. We had left the provincial park, ridden to Rossland and readied for a 700-metre high-speed descent into Trail. Throwing caution to the wind, I took my hands off the brakes and watched the speedometer on my fully loaded bike climb up to 74 km/h. Rick was just ahead of me, and we laughed gleefully at our own recklessness.

It was a moody day, with grey clouds hanging overhead. Our end-of-day search for accommodations led to the town's RV park, when the caretaker, who we knew only as BJ, set us up on two of the best sheltered spots.

The next day, we had a steep climb out of Trail and headed for Ymir, where we planned to camp in the yard of Danny and Rio – friends of Rick's. As we stopped for lunch in Salmo, the sky was fitful, gloomy – raining one minute and sunny the next. We downed a shot of whiskey at the Salmo Hotel and rode the last 10 kilometres to Ymir. Danny and Rio's house was an ancient clapboard structure the couple had rebuilt, with plenty of rustic enhancements in the interior. A neighbour named Svend came over to check on why there were four tents in the yard. That's what people in small towns do.

We took a day to rest. The welcome bright morning sun allowed us to empty out our saturated panniers so our clothes could dry. It was a catch-up day – laundry at Danny and Rio's, fiddling with the bikes, catching up on emails. By afternoon, we were ready to head to the Hotel Ymir looking for the eccentric old owner, who was rumoured to have an extensive art collection. We were about to find out just how incredible that collection actually is. I wrote this blog:

Ymir Hotel An Unlikely Sanctuary For Great Canadian Art

From the dated, wood-frame exterior, it would be easy to dismiss Hotel Ymir (pronounced 'why-mer') as just another ramshackle old remnant of British Columbia's mining heyday, relying on income from the eerie glow of video gaming terminals to eke out a marginal existence.

But stepping inside is a bit like diving down the rabbit hole.

Although its origins date back to 1896, this is not an old, broken-down piss-tank. The hotel where the ConnecTour stopped to visit is, in fact, a rich repository of some of Canada's finest artists accented by a random collection of artifacts gathered by the owner's travels around the world.

The owner is Hans Wilking, a former nursery farm operator on Vancouver Island, who will turn 89 in September. Since he acquired the former biker bar in this central B.C. near-ghost town in 2005, he has been slowly rebuilding and filling it with an art and artifact collection valued by some at more than $2 million.

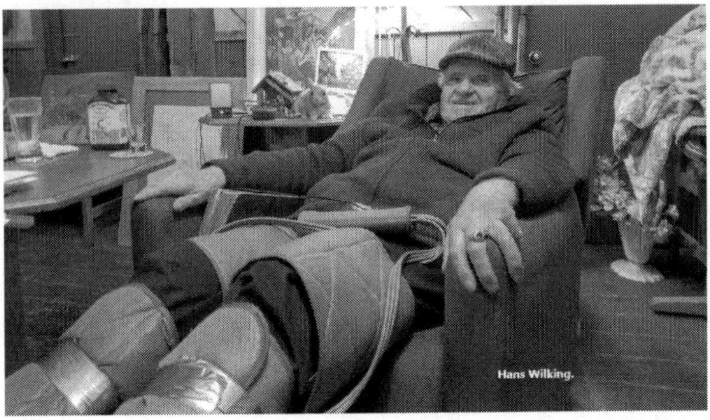

"Sixty years a packrat," he chuckles, as he sits in a recliner where he is giving himself a treatment to help ease the pain from two cracked vertebrae he received in a fall last winter.

During COVID, the lounge's main room is filled with large stuffed dolls – lions, kangaroos and bears – seated at tables that patrons would normally use. Yet, these are only a temporary distraction from the dozens and dozens of visual unicorns in every direction you turn your gaze.

By the door is an original painting by renowned Indigenous artist Norval Morrisseau, one of dozens of pieces in Wilking's collection. Because of COVID concerns, Wilking says we're not invited to view the gallery of Morrisseau's works decorating the second-floor hotel hallway; others are stored in a secure building in nearby Salmo.

Of the estimated 400 original paintings and artifacts are also works by Allan Edwards, E.J. Hughes, Richard Priest, Paul Ygartua, Marilyn Sunderman, and sculptor Simon Charlie. Many, like Morrisseau's works, were bought when the artists were relatively unknown. In fact, Wilking says he knew many of them personally, including Morrisseau when the artist was old and battling alcoholism on the streets of Vancouver.

"He was quite a character," says Wilking, with characteristic understatement.

The ceiling is adorned with hand-painted batiks from India that Wilking uses as sound-deadening. Carvings in the Pau Hana room include Salish works, as well as intricate masks and totems collected during travels he and his now-deceased wife Isabelle made to New Guinea and other nations in the South Pacific in the winter months when the nursery in Duncan was closed.

Behind it is the outdoor gnome garden, with dozens of the little creatures assembled around the showpiece carvings of two bears.

"I need to get out and oil those," says Gilles, the faithful carpenter who helped Wilking restore and expand the hotel and who now acts as both its bartender and manager. Rooms, he notes, still start at $59 a night.

There's also a collection of musical instruments that include a stand-up bass, a harp, an electric piano, an accordion, guitars and a banjo. These are not eye-candy . . . the pub has a Saturday night jam in which a lot of these devices are broken out by local musicians.

Wilking came by his collecting habit honestly. His maternal grandfather collected art, including early Picasso works, in a hotel in their native home near Bremen, Germany. That collection was confiscated by Soviet soldiers at the end of the Second World War and never returned, but the inclination to collect carried on with Wilking.

"We always collected art," says Wilking.

I ask Wilking what is the future for his beloved collection? He admits to some uncertainty.

"That's a good question," he shrugs. "I'd like to keep it all together."

Gilles says various art galleries have expressed interest in portions of the collection, but no one has shown interest in having it all.

For now, the only way to see this overpowering collection of works is to head over to Hotel Ymir, and buy a pint. It's unlike any pub you're ever going to see.

DRAFT-DODGER HQ

It's a relatively easy 30-kilometre run from Ymir to the hippie/ ski town of Nelson. I arranged to meet with Jo King, sister to a close friend I knew in Ontario, and her husband Phil Fertey for breakfast at the Vienna Cafe.

Phil, it turns out, loves eccentric bikes. He owns a penny-farthing that he had ordered custom-built. We planned to meet at their house so he can show off the bike, but Lisa and I were late getting out of Nelson and we missed them.

That night's accommodation was in a field owned by Warmshowers host Rick Greene, who has land near Balfour fronting on the Nelson River before it flows into Kootenay Lake. We took the ferry across the lake the next morning, stopped in at Barefoot Handweaving, owned by a friend of Rick's, and then set off for a vigorous 93-kilometre ride to Creston as storm clouds loom overhead.

Creston gets a bad rap. It's not far from the hamlet of Bountiful which is populated by members of two polygamist Mormon fundamentalist groups. The settlement is named after Bountiful in the Book of Mormon. Creston is a different kind of bountiful – it has a bounty of fruits and vegetables and the kind of friendly, rough-cut people you don't really see in cities. It's a prosperous little farm town with a flourishing agritourism trade.

The whole town feels a little bit like Letterkenny, except with gumption. We end up at the home of Warmshowers hosts, Jan and Zack Zacharias, a couple of anarchists who moved here from Dawson Creek after they retired. We set up our tents for the night in their massive front yard, surrounded by colourful flowerbeds adorned with hydrangeas and guarded by a pink llama statue, standing sentry by the front door. Next door is another Warmshowers host, Sheri Peel, who is a different kind of hippy but equally welcoming. She has an old school bus in her yard that she's converted into a camper, complete with a wood stove. Jenn decides to sleep there for the night.

Every day started with a plan. Some days we actually stuck to it. The next morning, as we exchanged hugs and thanks with our hosts, we were not at all sure we were going to execute according to plan. Our hoped-for destination was Moyie Lake Provincial Park, a 90-kilometre ride under off-and-on rain.

The past few days, I had become increasingly concerned about a nagging pain in my left knee while I'm riding. It seemed to be getting progressively worse and a knee brace did nothing to help. The group decided we'd go halfway to a hamlet called Yahk and see how we feel. After a treat at Two Scoop Steve's in Yahk, we decided we felt great and carried on. But by late afternoon I and my aching knee begged to stop in the town of Moyie, about 15 kilometres short of the park. Unfortunately, Moyie has no campgrounds, so Lisa and Rick headed off towards an old church in search of a yard in which we might be able to set up. And that is where they found Sherry Parsons, the ghost lady, standing on her porch beside the church.

Sherry Parsons with Rick

Sherry had keys to the church and invited us to sleep inside amongst the pews. Her friend Paul set us up with a toilet in a house across the street he was planning to tear down. It's eerie – a functional toilet sat in the middle of the interior with just bare studs where walls would have once afforded privacy. We set up a kitchen on the back of the church, and Sherry soon began to regale us with ghost stories. Here's what I wrote about that encounter:

Moyie's Muse Is Content To Live With The Old Mining Town's Ghosts

MOYIE, B.C. – Sherry Parsons lives in a home full of ghosts in an out-of-the way former mining town in British Columbia's East Kootenays. And she's OK with that.

Parsons, 74, and her husband, Michael, built a house next to the historic St. Peter's Catholic Church in Moyie, B.C., after struggling for years to gain title. Through a twist of travel fate, the ConnecTour group has landed at her yard looking for a place to stay.

Gaining title to the property wasn't easy . . . the former Fort McMurray resident eventually found the owner, Mary, the former madam of a brothel that operated on the site in the 1960s. Parsons chased her down at a bar in nearby Yahk and convinced her to sign over the title to the land in about 1985.

But here's the thing about the land. It was the site of the previous Catholic church in Moyie, and then it was a home of, as Parsons says, "ill repute" during Moyie's brief heyday of mining galena, a source of silver.

As was common in historic western Canadian mining towns, the rough-cut dreams of hard-drinking, get-rich-quick prospectors came up hard against the brutal reality of the "service industry" – young women pressed into prostitution at the behest of a merciless madam, who operated more like a slave-master.

The brothel in question, however, came much later . . . Parsons said a man named Gus Rudd won the building in a poker game about 60 years ago, and decided to turn it into a brothel. The madam also had some backup muscle, a big strapping man known as Bubba, who would be turned loose on the girls when they got out of line.

The women were angry and fearful of the enforcers, and the beatings that came their way if they got on the wrong side of Bubba.

Parsons believes the ghosts of those women have never left the place where they were forced to ply their trade. After Parsons and her husband built their home and moved in around 2005, they noticed something odd in their home – a presence that would set the pets howling in fear.

"It's haunted, definitely," said Parsons. "From the ladies of the evening. The church was dismantled years ago, and they put in a little brown shack."

It didn't take long to discover the ghosts in their home.

"The first clue was little wisps of smoke, but it wasn't smoke," said

Parsons. "It was a fog. And the animals immediately alerted us to it.

"And I knew, because of the history, and having a bullying madam, a mean bitch. And she said to me, 'The only time I sic Bubba on the girls was when they fought over jewelry or those boa feathers. Other than that, if they plied their trade in the way they knew how, I didn't have to send Bubba to beat them up.'"

Parsons says she doesn't fear the ghosts because she understands the spirits of these girls have "no place to go" after they've been bought and sold. These women stayed angry, "And very few prostitutes ever were successful."

Parsons found that the former madam, Mary, had no assets, and so she was determined to acquire the property. She said the legal wrangling to get clear title to three adjacent properties lasted from 1985 to 2003.

This is a compelling late-night ghost story for the six members of the ConnecTour group, who have landed here after a day in the rain. We were tired and looking for a dry place to stay, and Parsons offered the Catholic church which is only occasionally used for services.

Some of our group chose to sleep outside in tents rather than risk the ire of these troubled spirits. Two brave souls slept inside.

There was a vaudevillian quality to the human kindness that Parsons offered our bedraggled group, but it was as authentic as the freshly baked chocolate chip cookies and hot tea she brought over to us. The price of admission this night was to be entertained as Parsons retold the local folklore, spiced up with her own bits of folk wisdom.

She prides herself in being a tough old broad who takes guff from no one. To anyone who offends her, she warns, "I'm going to drop-kick you through the goal posts from life, from which you will never return."

For us, Moyie is no longer just another pointless side trip off the highway. It is a community steeped in history and in the spirits of those hardy pioneers.

That night, we were forced to pack up in the rain. As so often happens, though, the skies cleared as we rode towards Cranbrook, allowing us to shed our rain suits. With a rare tailwind, we got there in 2 ½ hours. After a relaxed snack at Hot Shots Cafe, we grabbed groceries and then took the Rails to Trails pathway on our way to a remote rural community called Wycliffe. Unlike the cursed Trans-Canada Trail, the Rails to Trails pathway is an utterly fantastic smooth, paved trail. Our minds wandered as we loafed along the trail, sheltered by a canopy of trees. I stuck a Canadian flag on my handlebar and thought of Tragically Hip's Wheat Kings.

Our destination is a ranch owned by Warmshowers hosts Angela and Doug Hurd about five kilometres off our route. To the east, the towering Fisher Peak pokes through the Rocky Mountains range, reminding us that we were approaching our next province. Angela and Doug's homestead felt like a B.C. take on Shangri-La. The centrepiece is a hand-built eco-home with a green roof and its own root cellar. But Doug built the massive shed first, for his work as a heavy-duty mechanic. As we devoured the delicious dinner of curried beef stew the couple made us, Lisa and I agreed that this is one of those places you could imagine yourself spending the rest of your life in.

The next morning, we said goodbye to Jenn who had to return to her job in Calgary and headed out for a relatively easy ride to Canal Flats. We ambled along a scenic dirt road through the traditional territory of the Ktunaxa Nation, and near the once notorious Saint Eugene mission and residential school – now operated by the Indigenous community as a golf resort. We make our way over to Highway 93, and around the hamlet of Skookumchuk come across a couple in an RV park, studying us with curiosity at our heavily laden bicycles. Looking for water, we stopped to chat with them. Slavko, there with his wife Connie and her moth Georgia, reciprocated with beer.

It's a hot, dry day and Canal Flats at first appeared to be on its last legs. We rolled by a fenced-in former sawmill and into a tiny downtown littered with dilapidated stores. It would later prove to be a preview of the half-abandoned towns that litter the prairies. But this one is different. Prosperity lurks just beneath the surface. That abandoned sawmill is now a bitcoin mine, delivering new revenue and jobs to the town. And as we headed north to our Warmshowers host home on the shore of Columbia Lake, we discovered beautiful high-end cabins, many of which are used as weekend getaways for wealthy Calgarians. To our amazement, we discovered our host wasn't even there but had left a note telling us where we could find the keys. No need to set up tents – the bedrooms and kitchen are ours; just clean up before we leave. We took the long wooden staircase down to the dock and plunged into the lake for some end-of-day relief from the heat.

4. TAKING STOCK

A REST GIVES US TIME TO ASSESS

Temporarily relieved of our rigid routine of setting up tents and scrambling together meals, we used the time to take stock. It's been less than three weeks, but we already felt as though we've been riding forever. We have gotten stronger and closer as a group, and we were beginning to get a sense of just how enormous this odyssey is. Lisa reflected on what the trip has meant to each of us:

By Lisa Monforton

We've only been on the road for 18 days of our 110-day ride, but we've racked up pannier loads of experiences — most of them fun and fantastic, others more of the physically exhausting and unexpected, crazy-weather kind.

From time to time, we'll compile a list of the highlights and lowlights and some bike-touring tips for anyone who plans to see all or part of Canada from the seat of a bike.

Highlights

First, we'd like to give big shoutouts to a collection of roadside caregivers who've been so kind to us.

We stopped at a private RV community for lunch on the lawn of the community's clubhouse, knowing we were on private property. But it was a scorcher of a day and there was shade and a picnic table. Ian saw us rolling in and at first seemed leery we should be stopping here. As we ate lunch, Ian walked over with a massive jug of water and a bag of ice so we could refill our bottles. "I didn't know what to do, he told us. But, he said to himself, 'I'm a Canadian so I should do something nice.'"

Heading into Trail, B.C., for the night on a cold and rainy day, we didn't have a campsite booked. Rick found one on the edge of town, and spoke to the manager, BJ, to see if we could tent there for the night. BJ was genuinely concerned for us, soaked in our gear. He kindly offered a site for three tents at no extra cost and threw a pile of wood into the deal. "I just want you to be safe and warm," he told us. As we left the next morning, BJ bid us safe travels and asked us to write to him when we got to St. John's, NL.

After an arduous day climbing a couple of summits, over 1,100 metres and getting caught in a frigid rain, we finally arrived at Nancy Greene Provincial Park, cold, bordering on hypothermia, and tired.

We ran into Annie who was worried about us, as we huddled in the overhang of a locked camp lodge. As a COVID precaution, the lodge was bolted shut. Annie grabbed her screwdriver and got the door open, allowing us to light a fire in the wood stove to dry out a bit. She came to check on us regularly to see how we were doing. Another couple, Bill and Elaine, a few campsites down, told us to come and get some of their wood, which they chopped for us before handing it over.

We've stayed with several Warmshowers hosts who have opened their homes and yards to us, including Jan and Zack in Creston, Chris Troy in Canal Flats and Doug and Angela in Wycliffe.

Individual Highlights And Tips

Andrew Hawes: *There are so many highlights, it's hard to just come up with one. The amazing experience of rolling into Moyie and finding Sherry Parsons, who had the keys to the church and let us sleep and cook inside, on what was going to be a rainy night. And, then the next day we rode into Canal Flats and stayed in the lovely cabin of a Warmshowers host overlooking Columbia Lake. Hot and tired we jumped in for a refreshing dip in the lake.*

Andrew's tip: Go on a ride like this with Rick McFerrin.

Lynn Marshall: *Staying with Angela and Doug in Wycliffe. They had a stew dinner and mashed potatoes ready for us after a long day on the road from Cranbrook, and then blueberry pancakes for breakfast. "It was like she was looking forward to seeing us,' says Lynn. Angela told us she was "paying it forward" after having been hosted on her own cycle-touring trips in Europe.*

Lynn's bonus highlight: Finding the ice cream shop – Two Scoop

Steve's – at the top of a hill outside outside of Yahk, B.C.

Lynn's tip: Always have warm socks and a jar of peanut butter.

***Rick McFerrin:** Finally getting on the road after 15 months of planning.*

Rick's tip: Be flexible, and bring what you think you need, knowing you can always leave behind or buy what you need along the way.

***Lisa Monforton:** The overall curiosity, questions and enthusiasm for our ride by random people we've met on the road.*

Tip: Learn to take it one pedal stroke at a time. And even though that hill ahead can look intimidating, just get into the zone and take it slow and easy – and get over it.

***Doug Firby:** The morning mist and the call of the loons on the lake at Nancy Greene Provincial Park.*

Tip: No matter how daunting things may look at any given moment, keep calm and carry on.

Lowlights

There haven't been too many "bad" experiences except for two we all agree on. The first would have to be the disappointment in a portion of the Kettle Valley Trail.

After starting the ride along the beautiful Myra Canyon trestles, the KVR quickly devolves, because it is poorly maintained and used regularly by ATVs, which destroyed the path all the way to Chute Lake. Potholed, rock/boulder-strewn, arduous sandy stretches and at times deep puddles the width of the trail. We all had our turns falling off our bikes. There were bruises and scraped knees, and we finally made the decision to cut short our day and stay at a rec site at

Chute Lake.

The second lowlight was the long climb up to Nancy Greene Provincial Park, where we got caught in a sudden downpour and a temperature drop to around 0 C. We were all frozen, bordering on hypothermia, our fingers so cold we couldn't unsnap our panniers to get at extra layers. With the others ahead, Lisa and Doug hunkered down in a rest area washroom to warm up for 20 minutes and put on more layers, and then made the last 5-km dash to the park. The happy ending was that the sun came out and fellow campers gave us wood and opened the park cabin so we could warm up around the wood stove.

We passed huge hoodoos at Fairmont Hot Springs the next morning, past Lake Windermere on our way to Radium. We had to earn those last few kilometres grinding up a slow, steady climb to a friend's cabin on a golf resort just south of town. This 'cabin' is bigger than many homes, and we planned to take a rest day there. We'd arranged to meet a reporter from the local Columbia Valley Pioneer the next morning to tell our story. As we talked about what we were doing, the reporter, Haley, became animated, asking more and more questions. By the end of the interview two hours later, we had made yet another friend. It's the bicycle touring effect – a great way to meet the better side of humanity. Here is what she wrote:

Connectour Stops Through Radium Hot Springs On Cross-Country Cycling Tour

By Haley Grinder

ConnecTour, a group of individuals passionate about "cycling and adventure," is taking Canada by storm this summer — one wheel at a time. The group is composed of "an eclectic mix of people" cycling eastbound across Canada. By Day 18, and just over 1,000 kilometres logged, they arrived at Radium Hot Springs, marking the completion of an eighth of their trip.

The trek was supposed to begin in Victoria in early May. However, constantly changing COVID-19 restrictions delayed the group's starting date and changed their departure to May 28 out of Myra Canyon — a spot about 30 minutes south of downtown Kelowna.

The location change meant they could not take part in the "typical tradition," in which cyclists travelling coast-to-coast first dip their wheels at mile zero in the ocean just off Victoria. Forced to modify the custom, the group dipped their tires into a frisbee filled with Okanagan Springs 1516 lager. The idea was courtesy of Jim Barr, CEO of ZenSeekers, an online magazine based in Alberta and British Columbia.

Firby says the bikes they ride are heavy duty and designed for touring long distances. They're equipped with sturdy steel frames and have extra spokes in the wheels to compensate for the excess weight — varying anywhere from 40-60 pounds per person. All cyclists are also decked out in reflective safety vests to avoid any potential accidents.

ConnecTour aims to make it to St. Johns by mid-October, and will finish the 135-day stretch by flying back to the west coast and biking to their starting point back in Kelowna.

Rick McFerrin, Lisa Monforton, Doug Firby, Andrew Hawes, and Lynn Martel were the current riders travelling through Radium Hot Springs. The group of five, ranging in age from 50-69 years, say it was an exciting first leg of the expedition, composed of mud, rain, snow and temperatures dropping to zero degrees with little-to-no warning during an otherwise sunny day. Despite the unpredictable weather, the team remained in good spirits, choosing to focus on their highlights as they encountered multiple acts of kindness — from offerings of tea and cookies, to shelter from the elements, and even much-needed places to sleep.

The journey will be over 8,000 kilometres in length and aims to combat the isolation brought on by the recent pandemic by seeking out, talking to, and connecting with real Canadians.

"People were feeling very disconnected from each other or all confined [to their] homes, can't go into the workplace, so there's kind of a loss of a sense of community," says Doug Firby, journalist and one of the core members committed to cycling the entire route. "And we thought this would be kind of a really great way to reconnect communities as we travel across the country. Just going from community to community, meeting people, [and] learning what they're all about."

Each member brings something unique to the team. Firby and Monforton both have backgrounds in journalism. Meeting new people, hearing different stories, and "constantly learning," drives them on their journey.

Lynn, an ex-accountant and speed demon on her bike, helps to ground the group every morning, instilling a ritual of what she calls a daily "sunshine prayer"— a morning check-in where everyone rates their mental and physical health on a scale from 1-10.

Rick McFerrin, who is one of the ConnecTour team with his wife Tanya and others, decided to transform their love for cycling into a lifestyle, founding Two Wheel View in 2000, and then in 2018, OnaVelo: a "boutique bike touring company." McFerrin has cycled over 100,000 kilometres in more than 43 countries but has always wanted to do a cross-Canada trek. A humble leader, he says, "I have tools in my toolkit to fix bikes, but I also have tools in my head to work with the group," stressing the importance of community building during such a trying time.

Andrew Hawes says the experience has been "completely transformative." As a Canadian special forces veteran who struggles with PTSD, Hawes stresses the importance of connecting with others in order to preserve one's own mental health, not to mention the positive effects physical activity has when battling unseen emotional scars. "There's so many great Canadians, all with interesting stories that we just need."

Hawes says he instantly gravitated towards McFerrin. "I've seen leadership in him and I follow him, and I'm telling you, I don't just follow anybody." The entire group has become quite close in such a short period of time.

Although, Firby and Monforton — partners for over 25 years — also have their own cause to ride. "Our son-in-law recently discovered he's going to need a liver transplant," says Firby. The pair wanted to bring awareness to the shortage of organ donations within Canada. Thankfully, as of June 29, they got the unexpected call that he had found a match. Expressing both gratitude and relief, they are "still riding for Dax," who has "many long and potentially difficult days ahead as he recovers from this major surgery."

ConnecTour is still cautious despite the worst of the pandemic seemingly being behind us. Having plenty of sanitizer on hand and doing regular morning temperature checks have become daily standards. The group remains inclusive to all, regardless of age or experience, leaving individuals or groups with the option to join for a day, week, month, or even the entire trip.

A Cynic Reconsiders His View Of Human Nature

Haley was waiting for us the next morning to take our photo at Radium's main intersection, where we would turn east and head towards Alberta on Highway 93. She came with gifts: cans of tuna, a jar of peanut butter, trail mix and little Canada key tags to inspire us along the way. I think about the many journalists I have known and worked with over the years and tried to imagine how many of them would have offered such a gesture. Here is a young reporter working for very little money and yet she felt compelled to contribute to our cause. It's the sort of generosity we would see again and again as we worked our way across the country. For the first time, it occurred to me that my dark, hard-nosed, cynical view of human nature – reinforced by decades of writing about criminals, cheats and dirty politicians – may have to bend to let a little light in. And I wondered: If you only expect to see bad people, then is that what you find? What then if you expect to see good people instead? Do you find them? Or do they find you?

What is not good, however, is the next 15 kilometres. No good rest day goes unpunished. I've driven this road a number of times and never really taken note of the long, steady climb out of Radium. Today, on my fully loaded Surly, I discovered just how relentless the climb is. We geared down and ground our way up an 830-metre gain. Stopping to rest at the peak of the climb, we met a family with a car, truck and loaded trailer who told us they were moving from Whistler to Stratford, ON.

It was a vigorous ride and we were happy to rent a cabin at the Kootenay Park Lodge. There, we found Paul Duffy and partner Dawn. They have an old Dodge van which they call Blue Lagoon, and have been on a tour of Canada with their beloved dog Mr. Kim.

Paul & Dawn with the Blue Lagoon

Paul is from Donegal, Ireland, and Dawn is from Horning's Mills, Ontario. They met in 2008 while teaching in Seoul, Korea, fell in love and decided to blow up their lives.

"We've literally been together ever since," said Dawn.

They tell us that, as COVID restrictions ease, they plan to move to Thailand. Hitting the road in a van was "the scariest thing we ever did," said Paul.

5. ALBERTA

FROM MOUNTAINS TO PRAIRIES

It was a cool morning at the Lodge, but sunny and clear as we started the long ride to the top of the Continental Divide and provincial border. Up here, the Rockies are moody, even slightly menacing, especially where forest fires have left mountainsides with charred debris where thick stands of spruce and pine once stood. We were about to reach the Alberta border and we felt a sense of accomplishment and profundity at what yet lie ahead. Nine more provinces to go. It still seems too great to contemplate, and yet the adventures of the past few weeks had given us an appetite for more. Heading down a steep and fast run to Castle Junction, we stopped for lunch and then took the quiet Highway 1A into Banff. This tourist town is normally overrun with visitors by this time of year, but Banff Avenue is still feeling the chilling effects of the pandemic. Only a handful of tourists wandered down the main street which is closed to vehicle traffic. We stopped for a beer on Banff Avenue, and soon started a chat with Robb Syre and Dallis Loran at a nearby table.

Dallis Loran & Robb Syre

It's been a tough couple of years for Robb who moved from Vancouver to Banff in 2020 to work at a tattoo shop founded by his best friend Ronnie Giesbrecht and an associate, Leighton Gall. "Honestly, at first I thought it (COVID) was total bullshit. It was just the flu, rebranded."

But then life took a sudden, tragic turn. Giesbrecht, Syre's best friend for a quarter of a century, contracted a severe case of the virus. Within five days, he was dead. It turns out Banff, with its transient population of young workers, was a hotbed of COVID. In April 2021, the health region stated that Banff and Lake Louise had the highest provincial rate of COVID-19 for its population size in April. Giesbrecht's death turned Robb's attitude about COVID upside down and motivated him to finally get vaccinated.

Syre, 48, grew up in Kelowna, and had been practising the art of tattooing for three decades. He and Giesbrecht hatched the plan to move from Vancouver to Banff in 2020. The two would sit together after work each day and chat about the business. "He was awesome," Syre said of Giesbrecht. "He would do anything for anybody, anytime."

I point to a grease spot the shape of a sprocket on my calf and ask him if he could do a tattoo like that. Robb laughed and said he would welcome the break from what he calls the Pinterest crowd – "wildflowers and grizzly bears" – themes that bore him so much he half-jokingly says he can do them while looking out the window.

We carried on to Canmore along the Legacy Trail bicycle path, heading to camp in the yard of Bruce and Gini, who are friends of Rick. That evening, Andrew and I ran into a young woman during a walk along the Bow River. She seemed lost – uncertain about what she wanted to do – but Drew told me later that he felt he had a special connection with her. I was confused by his attitude because I thought I saw a very shy, vulnerable person in her. As we headed east to the Ghost River reservoir the next day, Drew surprised us by saying he was going back to look for her. On this journey, we are all seeking something. I wonder to myself what hole in his heart Drew is seeking to fill and how he could possibly think a chance evening encounter might help him get there.

Two days later, we rolled into Calgary for a planned one-week break. Lisa and I were working on a video Seekers Media was producing for Destination Canada, and we needed several days for shooting.

I was grateful for the break because the pain in my left knee had become almost unbearable. It is inflammation caused by overexertion of the knee on those steep hills. For the last few days, I'd been using my right leg for power because I couldn't bear to put pressure on my left leg. I hadn't told the others just how much pain I was in.

More importantly, I hadn't told them that if it didn't improve my cross-Canada tour was about to come to an end. I vowed to spend the week with as little time in the saddle as possible to give the inflammation – effusion is the technical term – a chance to subside.

Back In The Saddle Again

Miraculously, the rest worked. By the time we headed north toward the hamlet of Irricana on June 26, the pain in my knee was almost entirely gone and I vowed that I was not done yet. Will it hold out for 7,000 or 8,000 more kilometres? Will I? I was going to take it one day at a time. I was actually feeling quite good – the fittest I have been in years and I was loving the fact that I could eat as much as I wanted – and what I wanted – and still lose weight. That alone seemed to be a good enough reason to continue.

And Then There Was Sid

Almost immediately, we found another great reason to carry on. We were about to enter a new chapter in our adventures. We decided to stop for the day at Irricana, a literal one-horse town (it has a statue of a horse outside the ramshackle Hotel

Irricana) and it also happens to have a municipal campground. Drew, who had rejoined us after a failed attempt to chase down the woman in Canmore, chatted up the campground managers, Sid and Louise Reid, while we set up the tents. As Drew often did through this trip, he discovered that these very ordinary folks had an incredible story.

Louise and Sid Ryan

Sid greeted me in navy blue shorts and T-shirt. I am immediately struck by his penetrating blue eyes beneath a tangle of white hair. He turned 76 in 2021 and has lived in two-thirds of our expansive country – and a literal lifetime – away from his home province. He and Louise were enjoying a simple retirement in Irricana, the peaceful denouement to a life that started with a cruel turn of fate when Sid was just a teenager in Newfoundland.

As he began to tell his story, an unmistakable Newfoundland lilt forms. Sid grew up on Bell Island, a 34-square-kilometre piece of rock a short ferry ride from St. John's, NL. Once a major mining community, it was the prosperous home to 18,000 people at its peak. But Sid never got the chance to enjoy the island's prosperity. He was just 15 years old, the second youngest of 15 children, when his father kicked him out of the house, penniless and directionless. Sid told us he had been out with two friends one evening, seeking mischief, and threw pebbles at a passing RCMP car. The police chased the boys and caught one, who named his co-perpetrators.

“When I got home, my father opened the door just this wide and asked me what I’d been up to,” said Reid. He told his dad he’d had a quiet evening with his friends.

“Well, my dad says, the RCMP have been here,” he said. His father knew the whole story.

Sid’s father was a fisherman who was “raised up hard,” and had no time for his son’s behaviour, which he found embarrassing. "You've brought attention to the family,” his dad told Sid. Then, he handed his son a paper bag with some clothes in it and told him to go.

He had nothing – not even the 10 cents needed to pay for the ferry over to St. John’s. He snuck on board, and a crew member who caught him took mercy and let him stay. Somehow, Sid was able to hitchhike to Toronto, where he found an uncle whom his mother had told him to look up. Once in Toronto, he found a job and saved money until he was able to move west and worked at the Carling O'Keefe brewery in Calgary. He met Louise while teaching two-step dancing at an old cowboy bar in Calgary. “I saw her walk in the door and fell madly in love,” said Sid.

The last time Sid was on Bell Island was 1992. His eyes misting lightly, he looked at us and asked a small favour. There’s a bar, he says, just off the ferry called Dick’s. He asked us to go there and have a shot of screech. “Say hi to Walter if he's still around,” said Sid.

We look at each other with tears in our eyes. We agreed: We had to get to Bell Island.

A LIFE-SAVING PHONE CALL

But our emotional roller-coaster had one more run planned for us. As we headed from Irricana to Drumheller on June 22, Lisa took a call she had both been hoping for and dreading. She recounts what happened next:

The call came out of the blue on a Tuesday afternoon. Our son-in-law, Dax learned there was a liver available and he was told to come to Vancouver General Hospital immediately.

Within 36 hours, the liver was declared a match and, just like that, Dax was undergoing the 10-hour surgery. This was thanks to someone who had taken the time and thought to be an organ donor. The average wait for a liver transplant in Canada is 287 days. Dax was one of the lucky ones – his wait was just a few weeks.

Dax has many long and potentially difficult days ahead as he recovers from this major surgery. We're riding for him, and for the cause of organ donation. Not everyone who needs an organ transplant will be as lucky as Dax was.

After a relaxing night of camping in one of Drumheller's dinosaur-themed campgrounds, we headed north out of town, found a set of scales, weighed our bikes (average about 60 pounds with panniers on) and then turned east with a strong sidewind that haunted us for the rest of the day. We were about to encounter one of the most cyclist-unfriendly places of the entire trip – Hanna.

Hanna. You know, Nickelback is from this prairie town. Chad and the boys don't come back too often, I'm told. When I'm on a bike, I won't hurry back either. Unlike the at-times almost rock star greeting we found at little towns we rolled into until now, Hanna's locals greeted us with at-best indifference and, occasionally, hostility. We pulled into the municipal campground at Fox Lake, one of the leech-infested sloughs that stretch from here to the Ontario border. The camp manager looked dismissively at our five bikes and told us the fee would be for five campsites. We argued with him: All of our tents would fit on the footprint of one of those big RVs these sites are made for. No, said the camp manager. Rick, our obstinate negotiator, responded, "What if we set up the tents in the shape of an RV?" The manager didn't laugh. Eventually, we sawed off on a fee for two campsites, and grumpily settled in for the evening.

OASIS IN A GHOST TOWN

And yet, as much as Hanna put us off, we were about to once again encounter life-affirming hospitality. The days were becoming incredibly hot, with mid-day temperatures soaring close to 40C. We were up by 5 a.m., and on the road by 6:30 trying to get a jump on the heat. We packed as much water as we could load on our bikes but by noon we were running out. For the first time on the trip, I began to worry that we might face serious dehydration. Allison and I were ahead of the pack when we came across a near-ghost town called Chinook.

There was a shed just off the road with a firehose hanging from it. It was a municipal water tank, put there to supply local farmers. A sign indicated that, for a loonie, we could get 50 gallons of water. Allison and I looked at each, shrugged, and then lined up every empty container we could find. We laughed hysterically as a flood of water came out of the firehose – way more than we could capture.

Eventually, we just stood under the hose and let it wash over us. It was wasteful, but it was also the best loonie we'd ever spent.

Chinook was our first view of what would be abandoned town after town in eastern Alberta and Saskatchewan, gutted by the shift to mega-sized farming and the flight of youth to cities. A former Ford dealership stood half-collapsed down the street. Old clapboard houses were boarded up and surrounded by weeds.

As the rest of the group caught up to us, we spotted a town hall that was tall enough to provide shade from the relentless sun. We rode over there and collapsed in the shade feeling a bit grim about the rest of the day. Our planned destination was a hamlet called Cereal another 20 minutes down the road. It appeared from photos that its campground was barren and treeless. As unattractive as it appeared in Google Maps, it seemed literally to be our only option. Fine. We'll rest here for half an hour and then push on.

Thankfully, Hank Gunderson had different plans for us. Here's what I wrote about the rest of that day:

Pool Party On The Prairie: Neighbourly Antidote To A Heat Wave

Canada's prairies have plenty of big sky and sprawling fields of wheat and canola as far as the eye can see.

What they don't have much of is water and shade.

A refreshing dip in the pool.

This week has been a record-setting heat wave, and it has been potentially dangerous for the ConnecTour bicyclists on a tour across the country. On Tuesday, we struck out from Hanna by 6:30 a.m., trying to beat the intense mid-day sun. The first two hours were golden, and we set a lively pace, but by late morning the merciless sun was taking its toll. No amount of hydration seemed to be adequate for the environment we were bravely soldiering through.

We had travelled roughly 80 kilometres by the time we arrived in the little hamlet of Chinook, Alberta – a once-thriving town that is now home to 11 households – and we took shelter beside the community hall. Allison and I were the first to arrive, and we found a municipal water supply that would dispense 50 gallons of water for one loonie. That was a deal that was too good to resist, and we refilled our bottles with the cool gift of life.

As the others arrived, we found the shady side of the community hall and laid out lunch. A couple of us, suffering from physical and heat exhaustion, laid down and passed out for a few minutes of respite. In turns out, grabbing that nap was a fortuitous move.

As we were preparing to remount our bicycles for a ride to the next town, we were approached by a Jeep Liberty. Out hopped Hank Gunderson, with a bag of ice in one hand and a dozen bottles of water in the other.

"Are you folks all right?" he asked, as we approached us. "You scared me there."

He said he had seen a couple of us laying on the ground and feared the worst – that a couple of us had experienced heat stroke. He was coming over to see what he could do. Such unexpected generosity is what makes this ride so exceptional.

We took Hank's water with thanks, but he wasn't satisfied. He insisted that we stop by his house so we could cool off under the garden hose before we continued our ride.

That's when neighbour Rick Brown stepped in. You're not really planning to head back out into this heat? he asked. "I've got a great campsite back here." It turns out he also had a backyard pool and was more than happy to share a few drinks and burgers over the barbie.

We looked at the thermometer above the pool. It read 39 C. It didn't take us long to decide our ride for the day was done.

On a long-distance ride, it is always possible to get caught in the "need-to" agenda. We need to be in Kindersley by Thursday. We need to stay on schedule.

But common sense also tells you that you need to listen to your bodies and not push them beyond safe limits. We took Rick up on his generous offer and pitched our tent under some shady trees for the night. There, we learned about his career in the military, what brought him to Chinook – a hamlet that is a long way from anywhere – and how people who live in small towns learn that every neighbour is their friend.

When it's minus 40 and the power goes out in winter – as it often does here – neighbours make sure you've got a warm place to stay until it comes back on. And that can be a long time. When strangers show up, and they look like they're overheated, you welcome them into your home. It's what caring people do.

Canada Day is about to be upon us. Somehow, I feel like what we have experienced here says so much more about Canada than some ceremony on Parliament Hill. I'm falling love with this country all over again.

We left again at 6:30 a.m. to beat the heat and found the barren campground at Cereal, just eight kilometres down the road. Thank God we didn't count on finding sanctuary there. By late morning, we confronted a blast of superheated air as we battled a headwind. Conventional wisdom is that the west-to-east tour is easier than the opposite direction because you often have the wind at your back. This year, however, broke the pattern – feeding us strong headwinds for most of our days on the prairie.

Yet, we were buoyed by the people we encountered. As we stopped for coffee at the Co-op at the turnoff to Oyen, some workers chatting with Andrew heard what we were doing. "No way!" one declared, his eyes growing wide in amazement. Looking for something to give us, he reached into his truck and handed Andrew a can of sunscreen.

The Seductive Cruelty Of The Prairies

Wind
flattening its gaunt furious self against
the naked siding, knifing in the wounds
of time, pausing to tear aside the last
old scab of paint.

Wind
surging down the cocoa-coloured seams
of summer-fallow, darting in about
white hoofs and brown, snatching the sweaty cap
shielding red eyes.

Wind
filling the dry mouth with bitter dust
whipping the shoulders worry-bowed too soon,
soiling the water pail, and in grim prophecy greying the hair.
- *From The Wind Our Enemy by Marriott Anne*

People who have only ever driven across the prairies on the Trans-Canada Highway will tell you that the scenery is tedious and boring. It is true that there are long stretches of land so flat that you can see a car that passes you for an hour. But in our experience, those Trans-Canada travellers haven't seen, felt, smelled and touched the real prairies. This is a place where the panoramic sky is like a head too big for its earthly shoulders. It's a place where impossibly blue skies can be invaded by menacing black clouds that deliver a dangerously chilling summer hailstorm. And it is wind. Relentless, energy-sucking wind.

6. SASKATCHEWAN

GHOSTS HAUNT DYING COMMUNITIES

As we crossed the border into Saskatchewan, the two-lane Highway 9 becomes provincial Highway 7. Within a few minutes, we reached Alsask – another town in its dying throes. The last bank – an RBC – closed three years before we got there, and the motel had been torn down. There's no grocery store and the streets are deserted. There is, however, a decommissioned military base which was built in1962 as part of the "Pinetree Line" network. This DEW (distance early warning) radar system was a joint Canada/U.S. project that aimed to detect Soviet long-range bombers during the height of the Cold War. As missile range increased, the DEW line was moved north to Canada's Arctic. The Alsask base was decommissioned in 1987, and 125 military personnel left town, as did another 60 civilian jobs. For the hamlet of Alsask, it was a death blow. The population dwindled from 800 at its peak to about 100 today.

The vacant skeleton of the 400-acre military base sent eerie chills down our spines as we rolled out of the moribund centre of town. Weeds were in advanced stages thrusting apart the base's aged asphalt. Where the residences once stood, only foundations remain. An old school which served as a senior's centre after the base was closed has been vacant since the 1990s, its windows broken and its main floor collapsing into the basement. Combing through the wreck, we found a table to use for the random campsite we set up on one of the lots of a former house. As we walked by the enclosed swimming pool, we were shocked to hear voices echoing inside. We discovered the town had preserved the swimming pool, and it is fully functional even now, complete with showers – such a rare treat in rural Saskatchewan.

Late in the day, our friend Jeff Wearmouth drove into our campsite. Jeff project manages the construction of wind farms and he had just finished a major project in the province. The back of his pickup was loaded with furniture he had brought with him to the job.

Allison relaxing in an overgrown military residence site.

We grabbed a large easy chair and set it up on the grass for an evening of beer-fueled giddiness. As we complained about the damned headwinds, Jeff said, "Don't you check Windy?" It's an app that predicts with annoying accuracy the direction of winds each day. From that point on, we used it to get a read on just how challenging the day might be. That is, until that moment, somewhere in Ontario, when we deleted the app because sometimes it's better not to know.

Headwinds are like hills, except worse. A hill can be measured. You know going in just how difficult a hill is going to be and the experience usually turns out to be pretty much as you expected. Headwinds, on the other hand, are fickle. Often, there is no headwind at all in early mornings, and then it sneaks up on you. And suddenly, you realize that you are putting in double the work for half the progress. But like those "dips", as Rick calls them, you just have to put your head down and not think about how many kilometres you have left in your day's ride.

JULY

On Canada Day, I posted the video of our lovely ride on the Rails to Trails ride in B.C., set to the tune Wheat Kings by the Tragically Hip, and the ConnecTour group set course for Kindersley. As Windy had predicted, we faced stiff winds from the southeast delivering a blast of 36 C air into our leathered faces. Over lunch at the Red Lion pub, we met Marion who has owned the local fixture for 40 years. Camping in the municipal campground, we were too tired to stay up for fireworks. The next day, we moved on to Rosetown, a community that is not only uncharacteristically prosperous in this province but is also home to one of our team member's family. Allison Flach remembered spending her childhood with her aunt and uncle there. It's a rest day, and we are grateful that is the day the skies opened up, giving some relief from the fierce heat. During a break in the rain, we wandered into an antique shop and stumbled onto another incredible story. Here's what I wrote:

Antique store owner revives memories for bikepacker

There's a leak in the roof at Riches Antiques that's filling the bucket in the rear left corner of this old store in Rosetown, but Sandra Mathison is unperturbed.

It's hard to keep shingles on the northwest corner, she explains, because that's where the prevailing winds come from. Today, those winds have brought in a long-awaited rain, a welcome relief from the heatwave that has been baking the midwest but maybe too late to save the crops.

Sandra, 69, continues to run the antique store with her 11-year-old pet Havanese dog, Duncan, even though she lost her beloved husband Rich three years ago. Born and raised in the area, Sandra and Rich were high school sweethearts and carved out a life for themselves and their five kids in Rosetown, after moving around the province for years while Rich was working for SaskTel.

This is an emotional moment for ConnecTour team member Allison Flach. She spent summers here as a kid, staying with her grandparents, Art and Beulah Flach. Her father, Peter, went to high school here and we learn from Sandra that she knew him.

Sandra Mathison

"He was in my husband's class (in high school), so he was a year ahead of me but, yeah, I knew Peter," she says.

Grandfather Art, it turns out, was an institution in town. He operated the town's movie theatre for many years before partnering up with Louie Boucher to run a store called Boucher and Flach.

It was revolutionary idea at the time, says Sandra, because a Catholic and a Protestant had never before paired up to operate a store. Until then, the two communities had been divided, but the establishment of that store changed people's minds about how the community could operate. "They went into business together, and all of a sudden it was, 'Huh! Well, if they can be friends and work in business, then the rest of us can get along fine.

"The town, it was very Ku Klux Klan back in the '40s,

"It changed the whole character of the town," says Sandra.

For teens, Boucher and Flach had a record listening booth, where customers could listen to records before they bought them.

"So in 1964, when the Beatles came out, you could go and pick out I Wanna Hold Your Hand. You went into this little room, and put the record on with headphones and decide whether you wanted the record or not. Most of us, as teenagers at that time, you just went in and listened to it."

The visit reawakened Allison's childhood memories of visiting the town.

"We loved coming to Rosetown. We'd get so excited." Coming back to town was "so nostalgic. I feel like I'm getting to know him on a level that I didn't know, 'cause he was kind of an older grandpa."

Grandpa Art died in 2008 at the age of 98.

"Everyone loved him," she says. In the family, "everybody strives to be like him."

MURDER IN MILDEN

The next day, a rare tailwind pushed us east towards Outlook. We turned onto Route 15 – one of the province's less-travelled roads – and within a couple of hours rolled into another shell of a town called Milden. In the centre of the village is a well-kept little park where the local retirees gather each morning for coffee and gossip. One of them, Ralph, told us about the latest town scandal: A transient woman who had taken a local man as a lover ended up killing him. The problem in this town, he said, is with the houses abandoned by people who have moved away and that become a target for squatters. With fewer than 150 residents, the village doesn't have the tax resources it needs to tear the houses down, he said. So, they stay there – decaying reminders of a time when the province was filled with such communities that became prosperous by serving the surrounding farms. As farms consolidated, the prosperity evaporated like a summer rain.

Ralph's story of murder was no myth. A records search revealed that Melissa MacQueen pled guilty in 2022 to a charge of manslaughter in the death of 61-year-old Randy Garrett the previous spring. (She was also later convicted of "repeatedly" sexually assaulting a person under the age of 16 in 2019.) Court was told MacQueen and Garrett had a volatile on-again, off-again relationship, involving heavy drinking. MacQueen attacked her lover with a hammer after they argued one night and he was found dead in his own home the next morning. By the time you read this, she will have served her time.

Gold Star Drivers

The secondary highways of Saskatchewan have rougher pavement than those on the two provinces to the west, but they are still a dream to ride. That's because Saskatchewan has not only the nicest drivers in the country but also the most considerate of cyclists. When approaching us from behind, those drivers almost always slow down, and when they pass, they move over to the oncoming lane so that we have as much room as possible. Drivers approaching from the opposite direction often move onto the far shoulder to provide as much room as possible. Their behaviour allowed us to relax and chatter with each other as we traveled down roads so straight they disappear into the horizon.

It was the middle of a sunny July day, searing hot as our voyage across Canada's prairie provinces had been. With its expansive and gently rolling landscape unravelling in slow motion beside us, a romantic like me would describe the scenery as genuinely Canadian as a William Kurelek painting; others might just dismiss it as boring.

We reached Outlook by noon, a beautiful surprise where the prairie drops into a stunning river valley with sandy beaches. We walked out into the river valley and waded into the cool, clean water, watching local children playing on the beach. Overhead was a high-level rail bridge, closed for structural reasons. (We later learned it is yet another broken link in the piecemeal Trans-Canada Trail). We spent the afternoon at the beach and then had a home-made Greek salad dinner. Feeling exhausted and lethargic, I turned in early. Little did I know how much I would need the rest to deal with the terror of the next day.

Like A Prairie Cloud

Two significant things happened the next day.

Drew, who had ridden with us from Princeton, told us he was

going to take a break from the group and strike out on his own. We said goodbye with mixed feelings; Drew was larger than life, moody, and self-absorbed. Too often, he would dominate our chats. But he was also our unofficial tail-gunner. He always rode at the back of the group, making sure everyone else was safe. There were times he would ride his Big Dummy cargo bike into the middle of the lane to force cars behind us to slow down. "I got your back," he'd say, recalling his days in the military. "No man left behind."

Today, of all days, we learned how much we would miss our tail-gunner, and how fate can intrude as quickly as a black prairie cloud. As we leisurely pedalled along the near-deserted road, we stopped at a canola field. I took a photo of Lisa and posted a cheesy Instagram: "Here's to a woman who's outstanding in her field." Were it not for a merciful twist of fate, it could have been the last photo I posted of her alive.

When something terrible and terrifying happens, there is a brief second – perhaps the time it takes a hummingbird to flap its wings once or twice – when you cannot process what you are seeing. Lisa's crash was just that sudden and unexpected. She and I were riding east on Highway 15 behind the rest of the team on this calm, sunny day. We had just cleared a section of the road where a crew was doing tar-and-chip surface repairs to the asphalt. Lisa sensed a vehicle approaching from behind and signalled that she was coming over to the shoulder. As she moved over, her rear pannier caught my front pannier. Losing control, she suddenly veered into the traffic lane. As I watched, I saw her front wheel go sideways and then she went down so fast and hard she didn't have a chance to put her hands out to break her fall.

I threw my gear-laden bike to the ditch and ran over to her. She was lying still on the pavement, entangled in her bike, eyes open but unresponsive. I called out to her once, and again, but she didn't respond. Fighting a sense of panic, I kept repeating her name. It could have been two minutes before she began to stir – I'm not sure. But she did, with her eyes blinking and her body struggling to sit up. By then, some passing motorists had gathered around. Someone called an ambulance, and learned it was a half-hour away.

At my request, a motorist had driven ahead and alerted the others in our ConnecTour group to the accident. Rick, Tanya and Allison made their way back to us and began the emergency protocols we had internalized before starting our cross-Canada venture. Yet even well-rehearsed protocols can't always account for the way humans will act under extreme stress. We had forgotten that you should never move an injured person if it's possible they've sustained a neck injury. As we – stupidly – slipped off her shattered helmet and sat Lisa up on a camp chair at the side of the road, it was obvious that her brain was scrambled.

"I don't remember what happened. Was I out?" she asked.

We told her about the fall and she nodded in agreement.

"I do not remember how any of that happened. What were we doing?"

Rick asked: "Do you remember where you stayed last night?"

Lisa looked down in confusion. "I can't remember even falling."

As the EMTs put on a collar and loaded her on a stretcher, I picked up her helmet and saw it was cracked into three pieces. I walked to the side of the ambulance and gave in to a rush of tears as our teammates gave reassuring hugs. The EMTs let me ride with them as we raced an hour north to Royal University Hospital in Saskatoon. Alive and conscious is a very welcome thing, but it was far from certain that Lisa was all right. Yet in this dreadful moment, I heard Lisa's familiar laugh from the back of the ambulance and felt a flood of relief as it became apparent that her brain was fully intact.

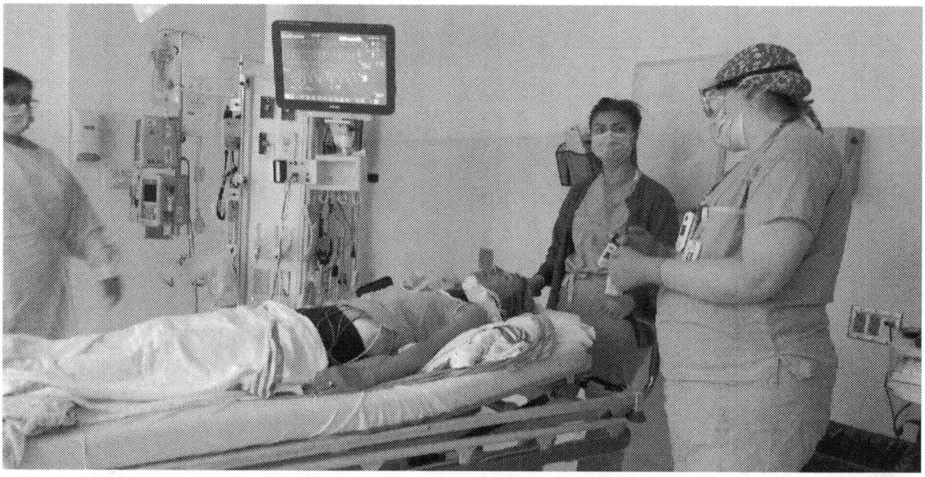

Two hours later, we left the hospital with Lisa's arm in a sling from a fractured clavicle. She also had a concussion and cracked ribs. Her ride was over – or so we thought.

I reached out to a fellow auto journalist I knew in Saskatoon – Jim Kerr, and he instantly offered to provide whatever help we needed. Meanwhile, the rest of the ConnecTour team had made friends with Tim Haugen, the driver who was approaching from behind when Lisa fell. After the ambulance left, Tim invited the crew over to his grandfather's farm nearby for lunch. And the next morning, he showed up at our Airbnb in Saskatoon with Lisa's and my bikes.

I asked Tim what he had seen of the crash. He shrugged the incident off as no big deal. "All my boys (three) have broken their collarbones," he chuckled. "They're full of pins and screws."

With Jim's help, we had Lisa's bike boxed within a day so that it could return with her to Ontario where she was to recuperate with her mom. Two days after the crash that scared the life out of her – and me – she boarded a plane for Pearson Airport in Toronto. It was an outcome that seemed almost too good to be true, thinking back to those terrifying moments after her crash.

Lisa told me she wasn't done with the ride. If she had enough time to heal at her mom's place in Windsor, she wanted to rejoin the ride. It seemed an impossible reach, but I wasn't going to tell her so. After I put her on the plane, Jim and his partner Deborah drove me an hour east to Watrous, so I could reunite with the ConnecTour crew. I fought back tears as we huddled together and shuddered at the drama of the last 48 hours. In two short days, our crew had been diminished by two core members. Then, we climbed aboard our bikes and headed east once again. As our venerable Surlys rolled along the broken pavement, our sombre mood gave way to the riding rhythm that had become as familiar as breathing to us. The Guess Who's Running Back to Saskatoon began to play in my head.

Stumbling On To A Legend

You have to be of a certain age to know that Kenny Shields was a thing. Somehow, as a Detroit-focused rock 'n roller in my teens, I had missed out on this Canadian music phenomenon. But there, as we rolled into the hamlet of Nokomis, was a billboard proudly announcing this was the home of the late rock star.

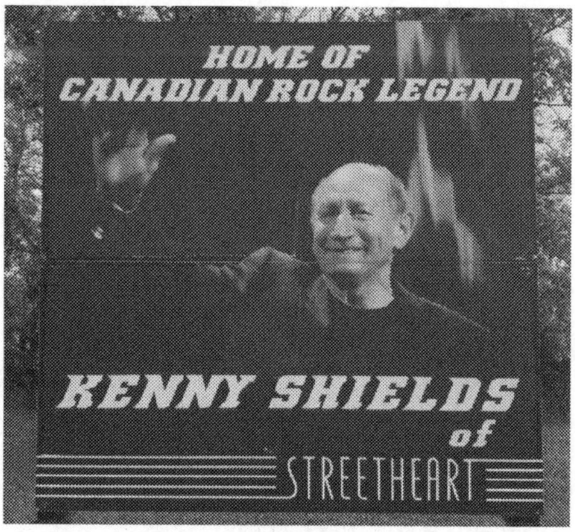

"Who the hell is that?" I scoffed as we rode by. Well, humility is a dish best served cold. A few months after we visited the hamlet, I posted a note on Facebook asking friends who knew Kenny Shields. As it happens, a lot of my friends grew up with the sounds of him and his band Streetheart.

Well! Just as Nickelback lifted the town of Hanna up from obscurity, Kenny Shields had done the same for Nokomis, a lovely and friendly hamlet of 450 near the dead centre of south-central Saskatchewan. Shield's band had some big days touring Canada during the 1970s, and even opened for such big-name acts as AC/DC, Styx and Canada's Max Webster. After two of his bandmates left to help form the band Loverboy in 1979, Kenny continued to perform until his death of heart failure in 2017 at the age of 69.

Now, Nokomis has a new claim to fame – one of the best breweries in western Canada. We turned into the drive of Nokomis Craft Ales and found Jeff Allport working in the back, surrounded by massive stainless steel kettles. He was initially cool to our presence – almost standoffish – until we started talking about his beer and what caused an Okanagan boy to move deep into the heart of Saskatchewan. He told us straight out he started his craft brewery in Nokomis because it was cheap to locate there. In fact, the town sold him three-quarters of an acre in 2014 for a buck and a promise to build there.

“I didn’t have much money,” he told us. “This has low cost of living and cheap land. And the water is really good here.”

Allport is sole owner of Nokomis Craft Ales, one of just a handful of rural craft breweries in the province. He said he struck out on his own because it was important to him to be independent, and not to have to rely on partners who might interfere with his vision. He brews quality ales that he sends across the province but doesn’t even have a taproom at his brewery. Instead, visitors who come from all over the province have only a collection of picnic tables outside where they can sample his beer.

“My focus is on brewing beer,” he says. “I don’t know anything about running a taproom.”

Jeff Allport with some of his product.

From tiny volumes initially, he has scaled up production to a still-modest 2,500 hectolitres per year. He only started canning his beers in 2018 and has just six employees. Bringing on a second brewer has given him the time to focus more on managing the business, although he insists on keeping his hand in brewing.

Raised in B.C.’s Okanagan, he was living in Vancouver before he started the brewery. Small-town Saskatchewan was a culture shock, he admitted, not only for himself but also for his partner Kara, who is an artist. To help ease the sting of losing that big city environment, the couple bought the local schoolhouse, which Kara has turned into a studio. Yet Allport admits to liking small-town life, especially the lower cost of living.

“Vancouver doesn’t offer a lot, in my opinion,” he said.

Allport sticks to simple local ingredients for his beers, eschewing “monotonous” trendy flavours, like chocolate stout. One of Nokomis’s favourite products is a barrel-aged farmhouse ale called Evening Star, a delicious sour that Allport says he makes no money on. He produces it because he wants to.

We grabbed a few beers and settled down at the picnic tables outside the brewery, grateful that even such a tiny hamlet could surprise us so.

We carried on to a hamlet called Lestock and that night camped in an empty yard near a muddy slough. Across the street from our camping spot is a church, closed as the population gradually disappeared.

On our way to Melville the next day, we stopped in Ituna looking for a pastry and a coffee. The server at a local lunch spot told us this is the only place in town – and pie is the closest thing they have to a pastry. Dissatisfied, we walked out and spotted a shabby looking store with its name – Zack’s – cut out in plywood in Rancho Western font, you know, the one you see in old westerns. Christmas lights hung over the clapboard exterior with peeling blue paint.

Inside was a potpourri of tchotchkes, ranging from plastic trinkets to fireworks. The Asian server, who we learned was the owner, barely spoke a word as he made coffee for us behind the counter. It was so good, we asked

Yong: Enjoying Canada's freedom.

him to step outside so we can do an Instagram post of him and his store.

It was at that moment that he began to relax and tell us his story. His name is Yong, and he is from the Wuhan province in China, the region where the COVID-19 virus originated.

He moved to San Francisco first and then decided to come to Saskatchewan in early 2020 when a friend told him about a little variety store that was for sale in this remote rural town. He told us he loves Canada because people are free to criticize the government or think whatever they want. In China, he said, there are no such freedoms.

Yong said the town has been very welcoming to him and he wanted to stay there. As we mounted our bikes, Yong came out with two packages of fireworks. They're not selling, he explained, so he wanted us to have them as a gift.

By the time we reached Melville later in the day, we'd travelled nearly 100 kilometres. The next day is a rest day, allowing us to buy supplies at the Canadian Tire, grab lunch at the local dive bar, wash our smelly cycling gear at the laundromat and grab some free wifi at the library. It's a quiet town. But that evening, on a beer-fueled whim, we set off the fireworks in a field beside the campground. We giggled like 12-year-olds, but no one in town seemed to notice or care. Maybe they were happy just to have a brief respite from the solitude.

The next day, I felt a sense of melancholy as we prepared to leave this province and head to our fourth – Manitoba. Much of what I thought I knew about Saskatchewan had been turned on its head. There are two ways you can view its endless straight roads and sprawling canola fields. People who drive through on the Trans-Canada Highway talk about the trip across Saskatchewan as a tedious exercise best slept through. We took the smaller roads and found something quite different; a province that represents the hardiest and most resourceful of Canadians, where generosity is as common as the canola fields, and where you can't afford to have enemies because every neighbour is expected to be there for the next. In the shadow of rich Alberta, Saskatchewan is the poorer but proud cousin that still understands what community means, even as its near-abandoned hamlets struggle to keep the lights on. It's been a magical eye-opening experience.

We headed east on the crumbling Highway 15 until it ends just south of Bredenbery, forcing us onto the much busier Yellowhead which would lead us into Russell. Russell the Bull, the town's mascot, is waiting to greet us as we roll under the arches that cover the downtown main street. The campground is barebones, with no potable water and mostly no trees. But we have learned there is always a way to adapt; we find a shady spot at the southern end of the campground and get water from a nearby business.

7. MANITOBA

TREASURES HIDDEN IN THE TREES

With a long day ahead of us, we decided we will make a choice when we reach Shoal Lake whether to press on to Minnedosa. At the moment, I didn't really care. It was exactly one week since Lisa's crash, and the three-person tent I normally share with her is feeling big and lonely. I eventually started to sprawl my stuff throughout the tent but there is still an aching loneliness. Yet today, we are having the best ride of our entire tour. With the first real tailwind since we left Kelowna more than six weeks ago, we were on track to complete 140 kilometres in one day.

To pass the time between conversations with fellow riders, throughout the trip I invited earworms into my head. As my mood shifts throughout the day, the tunes shifted from jumpy songs like the ones they use to pump you up at the gym to classic hits to offbeat and esoteric music performed by artists I can barely remember. Sometimes, I remade the tunes in my head – adding orchestral arrangements, soaring guitar riffs or new verses. Yet by the time we stop for the day, I can never remember these inspired arrangements.

This day, I broke into an ear-assaulting rendition of Christopher Cross's Ride Like the Wind:

It is the night
My body's weak
I'm on the run
No time to sleep
I've got to ride
Ride like the wind
To be free again

The rest of the team, showing remarkable tolerance, let me carry on.

We left Russell, Manitoba, thinking we would be doing well to reach Shoal Lake about 75 kilometres away. Instead, with the help of the wind we had reached Shoal Lake by 10:30 a.m., and we agreed Minnedosa – another 65 kilometres down the road – was well within our reach. We grabbed coffee at the Shell station. At the grocery store, as we were picking up apple fritters we ran into an old-timer on the street who told us he moved back from Courtney, B.C., because that town was too hectic for him. Shoal Lake, I thought, is certainly not.

KILLER BEES TRACK US DOWN

We knew Minnedosa has a large fresh-water lake, full-service campground and Winnipeg craft beer. We were determined to get there and have some afternoon fun. But a swarm of angry bees had other plans. Just about 15 kilometres from town as we flew along at 30-plus kilometres per hour on the wings of a powerful breeze, a swarm of bees madder than hornets emerged from seemingly nowhere. They were headed straight for us.

Tanya was leading the pack and encountered them first, coming at us like a fleet of enemy fighter planes.

"They started just hitting me," Tanya said. "It was kind of like a cloud of bees and they were just whacking me."

She decided to ride as fast as she could in the hope she would get past them. I was right behind Tanya, and felt them begin to hit my face, arms and chest like pebbles. I put my head down and heard them bouncing off the helmet. From behind, I heard Rick shout at Allison, who was at the back of the pack, "Keep going," but it was too late. One of the angry bees have found Allison's neck and let loose its stinging fury.

Allison's bee sting.

"Things were hitting my face and body, but I didn't really know what they were," said Allison. "It was like science fiction."

As the frenzy subsided, Rick stopped to tend to Allison. He got the stinger out and applied antiseptic and then we carried on into town.

What set those bees off? Why were they targeting us? Was it just a random coincidence or were they looking for something or someone to attack? Rick said that in all his world travels over more than two decades, he's never seen anything like it. The natural world has funny ways of expressing its displeasure.

Yet the day did end up being all we hoped it would be. Minnedosa is yet another prairie surprise, a prosperous town hidden in the inviting valley of the Little Saskatchewan River. Our campsite was beside Minnedosa Lake, the first real fresh-water lake we've seen in days, and we swam and stayed up late.

The shorter riding days are often harder than the longer ones. We didn't start the 75-kilometre ride to Gladstone until after 9, fueled by coffee and a jam-filled doughnut from the Minnedosa Cafe. In Neepawa, we found the great Farmery Estate Brewery, bought a few beers, and stopped in a town park. Those luncheon beers, however, added lead to our feet as we slogged toward Gladstone. There, we witnessed closeup the lengths local folks will go to in the war on mosquitoes.

We set up our tents under the shade of the mature trees of

the municipal campground. As we were finishing up dinner, a town employee came by and warned us to take shelter. After years of asking, the town had finally gotten permission to spray the entire area with the insecticide Malathion, and they were coming by our campsite in a matter of minutes. We stashed the dishes and ran across the road to watch the spectacle from upwind. As the sweet stench of the insecticide lingered, a quick Google search told us this: "Malathion has been reported to cause skin irritation and sensitization. Because it is readily absorbed through the skin, skin contact can result in systemic poisoning." We stayed out of the tents as late as possible.

At the end of the day, Rick got a note from Drew, announcing he would not be returning to the ConnecTour team. Rick and I had known the day would come when Drew would want to test himself on his own. As he recovered from his battle with substance abuse, he wanted to prove that he could cut it on his own. The ConnecTour group was like a crutch to him and he was ready to taste some independence. Rick and Drew exchanged texts:

Andrew: Just made it into Montmarte at the campground. There was no one here to help but a farming couple let me pitch my tent by their big trailer. And I going to go see their farm in the morning:)) crazy day ... wind was brutal...I imagine you had the same south to north winds

Rick: We had the same winds. Did 115 km today. Everyone has gone to bed now. I'm doing the same soon.

Andrew: I'm in Stoughton, Saskatchewan, area, helping a farmer and his family I met a few days ago... just going with it... long story ...still gonna do the cross country ride but obviously taking my time ... Just sorta happened.

Rick: Sounds like you are making your way.

Andrew: Always hoped there was something for me in Saskatchewan. Actually drove tractor yesterday, too.

We're out by 7 a.m. in hopes of beating end-of-day fatigue. The sun is already red and warm, and we hustled at a steady pace until we reached Portage la Prairie, where we stocked up on groceries and liquor. To our surprise, there was a security guard controlling admission to the liquor store. He explained the store has been hit by robberies, so the company takes the ID of everyone who is admitted. It is a jolting reminder that small towns are not as bucolic as city dwellers seem to think they are.

A Hidden Sanctuary

We carried on to our destination at Poplar Point, a crossroads a few kilometres northeast of Portage and found our Warmshowers hosts Ross and Brenda Bond. As we crossed the country, we found Warmshowers hosts as varied as the ever-changing geography – from warm and hospitable to cool and aloof, with homes that are in some cases elegant and pristine and in others dilapidated and, well, filthy. The Bonds' homestead was one of our favourites – with friendly and engaging hosts and a magical middle-of-nowhere sanctuary. The old yellow clapboard house sits about a kilometre south of Route 26. Beside it is a berm that separates the property from an oxbow that used to be part of the Assiniboine River. As recently as 2011, the river's banks overflowed and flooded the local farms, but now the oxbow is bone dry as a result of the drought plaguing much of western Canada.

Ross Bond in his workshop.

Of the many shady trees that keep the property cool, one in particular stood out. It's a mature elm that has managed to avoid the Dutch elm disease that has virtually rendered the species extinct in eastern Canada. Last year, Ross ponied up $800 to have the tree treated in the hopes of keeping it healthy.

Ross and Brenda bought the property in 1975 and slowly added to the house and outbuildings. Not far from the house is an old frame one-storey building that was once a United Church and, Ross has been told, served as a barracks for Japanese Canadians detained during the Second World War. He bought the building decades ago for $500, and today, it is filled with saws, planes, drills and a cornucopia of woodworking tools that Ross uses to ply his craft as a fine carpenter, making beautiful cabinets and furniture. He is soft-spoken and modest but does let slip that he once did work for a member of Winnipeg's Richardson family, whose juggernaut company built its wealth over a century-and-a-half in the grain, agri-food, energy, real estate, finance and transportation industries.

Brenda, though past retirement age, still works part-time in Winnipeg hospitals, providing spiritual counselling to patients. The Bonds joined Warmshowers the year before we arrived there, after their daughter Muriel rode her bicycle from Montreal to Manitoba and stayed with these hosts whenever she could. Mom and dad thought they should return the favour and became hosts. Besides, Ross and Brenda admit that it sometimes gets pretty quiet on the farm.

The wildlife in the area can be annoying. Beavers have invaded the pond which Ross's hand-built sauna overlooks. They're chewing through the trees and burrowing into the berm. Ross told us there are also feral pigs in the area, offspring of animals that escaped from a neighbour's farm years ago. Ross says one person claimed to have killed a 400-pound pig; himself, he felled a 100-pound animal. Many more are still on the loose.

Our night at the Bonds ended with a trip to Ross's sauna, heated to a searing temperature by a wood-fired stove. It's a perfect end to a visit with the two of the most engaging and generous Canadians we have encountered.

W.R.E.N.C.H.ing in Winnipeg

From Poplar Point, it's a straight shot into Winnipeg. We once again sought routes that would keep us off the miserable Trans-Canada and found ourselves winding through the affluent old-money district of Wellington Avenue, with its massive canopy of trees and car traffic restrictions. We've rented an Airbnb in St. Boniface, and planned to take a day off to run a bike clinic with a local bicycle charity called the W.R.E.N.C.H. (Winnipeg Repair Education 'N' Cycling Hub).

As not-for-profit cycling groups go, the W.R.E.N.CH. is in a highly evolved state. With funding from the federal government, community foundations and donors, it has grown since its founding in 2010 to a staff of 15, plus additional people who build bikes from recovered discards. Paid staff is bolstered by an army of 35 volunteers. The W.R.E.N.C.H. stores hundreds of bikes and various parts in a large garage in the city-owned building it occupies, said Gregory Allan, education coordinator. The intention is to get as many of those bicycles into good working order as possible, and then get them into the hands of young people who otherwise wouldn't be able to own one of their own.

The idea, said Allan, is to empower youth and other members of the community to engage in healthy living practices, develop useful skills and build self-confidence. Its programs include Earn-a-Bike, a series of workshops in which participants rebuild a bike, and then get to keep it; Youth Bike Builders, which trains youth bicycle maintenance; and outreach workshops, which are conducted with schools, community centres and youth agencies. There is also a program called Just Cycle, which supports kids who find themselves involved in the justice system, says Allan. And the group used funds raised from selling rebuilt bikes at its outlet at The Forks to support its programs.

Andrea with her repaired bike.

Today, however, we have set up a bicycle clinic on the grounds of Manitoba's legislature in the heart of downtown Winnipeg, fixing bikes for free just to build some community goodwill. As we set up, we heard a loud bang coming from the vicinity of where Donald Street crosses the Assiniboine River.

W.R.E.N.C.H. member Kevin Celestino quickly realized a bicycle tire had blown, and he headed off in a sprint to help out. Two minutes later, he's back with a young woman named Andrea, a shredded tire, and a bicycle that looks like it's been picked out of a landfill. Andrea is impatient to get her bike going because she is late to meet up with friends. But Kevin has to zip home to find a tire and wheel that will fit her bike.

By the time we're done, Andrea has a new tire and a new wheel mounted at no charge to her. The seized gear shifter will have to wait for another day. "You guys have saved a life," she smiled. The W.R.E.N.CH. has won over one more fan in a city that seems to have taken a shine to urban cycling.

Over the next two hours, we lubed chains, changed tires, adjusted derailers, straightened parts, fixed brakes and educated bike riders on how to do basic maintenance on their machines. Then, we sat down with a small group of adventure-seekers to tell a few of the stories from our nearly two months on the road.

We ended the day with cocktails at the Hotel Fort Garry and dinner in St. Boniface before we spent our last day in Friendly Manitoba. Lunching outdoors the next day at The Forks, we struck up a conversation with a group sitting next to us. One of them, John Lycar, told us he is also from Bell Island, NL, just like Sid Reid in Irricana. And yes, he knew of the family.

Plotting an exit that will keep us away from Highway 1, the next day we left Winnipeg via Dugald Road, past some light industry buildings. Once again, the geography shifted dramatically within a few kilometres, from prairie to Canadian shield. A hot crosswind slowed us as we ground past tree-lined fields with rocks popping through. By the time we reached the hamlet of Elma, we were ready to stop by the rapids on the Whitemouth River for a lunch break. But we are not to be left alone.

John: You're staying here.

A retirement age man drives up on his Arctic Cat ATV and we told him our story. "Of course, you're going to camp here," he said. We had planned on riding much further that day but had also learned never to turn down an invitation. "Get set up and then come over to my place for some beers." There, we met his brother Steve who was a former driver of a tractor-trailer and he told us stories about driving up icy hills in the winter. John had an early '60s vintage MGA A restored beautifully. He told us he had driven it to Florida and other areas of North America.

We camped under some evergreens where we hung some food away from animals. Unfortunately, we didn't realize the food was also hanging almost exactly above Allison's tent. When Rick got up in the middle of the night, he found a black bear cub trying to reach the food and shushed it away. Allison slept through it all.

8. NORTHERN ONTARIO

FIGHTING TO STAY AFLOAT AS TOURISTS LAY LOW

Half rock, half water and no soil. From an agricultural point of view the land is useless. From the point of view of a canoe trip aficionado, a fisherperson, a hunter, bird watcher, a geologist, a lover of lake swimming and anatomical rocks; it is paradise.

- *Joanne C Wittstock on Quora*

Ontario has something like 250,000 lakes. In northern Ontario, it felt like we rode by half of them.

It's easy, and probably more accurate, to think of Ontario as two provinces. There is the area that everyone knows in the south, that densely populated industrial/commercial belt that stretches from Windsor in the west along the frantic Highway 401 to the province's eastern border just a few kilometres from Montreal. And then, there is the north – a massive, mostly wild expanse of endless trees and Canadian Shield that many Canadians never get to. It is an astonishingly vast province – bigger than France and Spain combined and more than three times the size of Germany. We will have traveled more kilometres crossing this province than we did to reach across all three prairie provinces. Even figuring its modest-sized cities, like Sudbury and Sault Ste. Marie, northern Ontario has fewer than one million residents – less than one person per square kilometre. Southern Ontario, on the other hand, has nearly 14 million people and 118 people per square kilometre.

See what I mean? Two solitudes.

We entered Ontario, our fifth province, with no intention of riding 130 kilometres on the first day, but Tanya woke up with an eye infection and we had to get her to a clinic. We could either ride to Kenora or backtrack to Winnipeg, but we were loathe to go backwards. As we finished packing up, a thunderstorm blew in. It took about 20 minutes to subside and, by then, we were drenched. I was in a foul mood.

The land was scrubby, and very different from the prairie we had become so accustomed to. We were getting our first taste of the rises and falls that would soon turn into the full-scale hills north of Lake Superior that strike terror into the hearts of long-distance cyclists. As we rode, we found Sid's roadside truck stop tucked into a wooded area and stopped for burgers and fries. Crazy Sid is known for his massive French fries, and they were delicious. It fueled us for the final 30 km to Kenora, where Tanya got into the Two Doctors clinic – which, ironically, was entirely virtual. The drops and antibiotic offered almost immediate relief.

Ontario's forest fires were raging and had cloaked the town in a cloud of smoke so thick we could barely see a city block away. Kenora Bay, which normally provides a beautiful backdrop to downtown Water Street, was invisible. There was no escape from the soot that was making our eyes burn and our breathing heavy. At a loss, we decided to carry on and check out our warm showers host at the edge of town. It was a fortuitous turn. As we climbed a steep hill to Jake Boutwell's home the smoke thinned. The hill had put us above the smoke, allowing us to marvel over Jake's parents' massive, three-storey house. We threw together a dinner of tomatoes, veggies, eggs and left-over fries from Sid's.

We quite literally had reached a fork in the road: At Kenora we could take the fast and busy Trans-Canada Highway east on Highway 17 through endless boreal forest and limited scenery or turn south on Highway 71. It would take us deep into Lake of the Woods territory on a longer but more scenic route.

Naturally, we took the road less travelled into a part of Ontario that remains a magnet for hunters and sports fishers and that feels as though time has forgotten. Riding under overcast skies, we rolled into Sioux Narrows by early afternoon.

Rejecting an old, closed fishing lodge as a camping spot, we rode to the Tomahawk private campground just south of town, delighted to find showers that were as clean as any we had seen on the trip.

'You Make Sacrifices'

The next day, my birthday, we had a short ride to Crow Lake where Rick's friends, Courtney and Dawn, had rented a fishing cottage. It had started raining, and Courtney and Dawn mercifully offered us beds in the cabin, which we gratefully accepted.

Jake Tinkner: hanging on.

I wandered down the waterside shed to interview the lodge owner as he cleaned the day's catch. His name was Jake Tinkner, and within a few minutes of idle chatter, he relaxed into telling his story.

Jake was just 13 years old when his father bought a small fishing lodge on Crow Lake's Muskie Bay. The father moved his family from Minnesota and set out to pursue a dream of hosting anglers. Mom and dad, Paul and Christine Tinkner, ran the lodge for decades before easing back and slowly handing the day-to-day operations to Jake and his wife Ashley. The parents still run the other family resort in Whitefish Bay on Lake of the Woods. At both lodges, days are spent cleaning rooms, taking guests out for day-long fishing excursions and delivering their cleaned catches to them.

Although the long-term plan has been for Jake and Ashley to take over the entire family business, the couple, in their mid-30s, were facing an existential crisis because of business lost to the COVID-19 pandemic. Located just 120 kilometres north of the border with the United States, Muskie Bay has thrived – like most of the other area lodges – by catering to sport fishermen from the U.S. But when the border was closed in 2020, the Tinkners saw the majority of their customers disappear overnight.

"Ninety per cent of my business is American fishermen," said Jake, as he finished cleaning a day's catch for Courtney and Dawn. Tinkner said his family cut expenses to the bone and were scraping by with government financial assistance. "It's been tough," he said. "We've been living on pennies."

Yet the couple are not ready to give up on their idyllic home, which they hope to one day pass along to their two sons. The Tinkners have added amenities, such as a new sauna, with the goal of turning the resort into a year-round destination. If willpower counts for anything, it will be there and thriving once again when the next generation is ready to take it over.

"You make sacrifices to live the life you want," says Jake.

You do indeed.

That evening, Courtney and Dawn shared their day's catch with us – a huge stack of fresh crappie, bass and walleye – and I hoped the Tinkners would find a way to navigate through this dark, tough time.

We left Courtney and Dawn's place at Crow Lake in the rain and rode into Nestor Falls to buy groceries. As we rode south toward Emo, grey skies hung over the starkly beautiful landscape like a furrowed brow. Riding into a crosswind, I felt weak and tired and struggled to keep pace with the others. The skies had mostly cleared by the time we finally broke for lunch around 1:30. The only convenient shade was a huge solar panel and we stretched out on the concrete base as the panels pivoted with the sun's movement. We slept for an hour and then headed south past farmland with piles of hay bales in the fields to Rainy River, and then east again towards Emo where we planned to camp. With no campground in town, a server suggested we head to the soccer field which was equipped with both power and water. It was Tanya's birthday, and we cobbled together a dinner. No one seemed to care about the handful of tents set up in the soccer field.

The trip to Fort Frances the next day was just 40 kilometres, and we were excited by the prospect of staying at the lakeside home of Cam and Rita Moorhouse. Cam is brother to John, someone with whom we had ridden bikes in Argentina.

As we headed toward Fort Frances, my mind once again turned to Lisa. Even though we talked nearly every day, I missed her badly and felt lost in our suddenly oversized tent. She's a fan of Dave Matthews, and as we rode I realized my earworm was Stay Beautiful Lady. I'm sure she'd be pleased to know that. Fort Frances is a former woodmill town that sits right on the U.S. border.

We stopped for lunch at a little pub right downtown. A short woman with loose grey hair approached me as we were about to enter the pub and asked what we were doing. We're riding our bikes across Canada to get help people get reconnected, I told her. She told me her name was Norma, and she hesitated shyly and pulled out a $50 bill. "I want to buy you lunch," she said. I look at her incredulously, thinking that $50 is a lot of money for her to give away, but she insisted. I brought her inside and introduced her to the group, feeling deeply moved by her gesture.

Norma meets the ConnecTour crew.

The welcome at Cam and Rita's was even warmer. Even though we had never met, Cam told us not to bring a thing – dinner, drinks and our creature comforts would be taken care of.

A wild storm was blowing up as we arrived, and Cam helped us get the bikes into the garage. The house sits on a cliff overlooking Rainy Lake. In the living room is a grand piano that Rita plays, and I declined her invitation to play Beethoven's Fur Elise. I'm out of practice. Over dinner, Cam apologized – he's the on-duty physician and when the phone rings he'll have to answer it. He's helping a family member deal with the fact that his mother is dying – maybe that day. Cam calmly and compassionately talked to the family member and deftly switched back into entertainer mode when he hung up the phone. I wondered whether there will be another generation of doctors like Cam, willing to live in small towns with limited medical facilities, and yet carving out full and rewarding lives. We took the next day off so Cam could take us out on Rainy Lake in his speedboat to Windy Point, about

15 kilometres away. The sunny midsummer day is one of those you wish could go on forever, leisurely cruising in his boat to an almost deserted beach.

Refreshed, we left Cam and Rita's on July 24th without a definite destination in mind. At about 85 K, we spotted Branch's Seine River Lodge and stopped in to sample the product of their brewery. The lodge owners are Quentin and Lori Branch. Quentin is the son of people who bought the lodge in 1967. I thought about the Tinkners' struggle and asked Quentin and Lori how they were coping with the loss of business from the pandemic.

Quentin said when the lodge lost 98 per cent of its business — American fishermen — during COVID, the couple doubled down on their short-order meal service and started brewing their own beer. It turns out there is little competition in the area for good food, so locals will drive from as much as an hour away for a meal at the lodge. I was surprised to see that on this July evening, the restaurant and patio were alive with area visitors. The restaurant business is doing so well, says Quentin, when the U.S. travellers finally do come back, "We'll have to see how it will all fit in."

Quentin and Lori Branch

The couple also upgraded their lodge from the traditional rough style that appealed to sport fishermen in the past. Now, rooms have hotel-grade mattresses, more privacy, wifi and even colour TVs. Lori says that's what contemporary guests expect.

We camped for the night on the lodge's grounds with a cyclist named Sam, who told us he is riding from Vancouver to Gaspe. In the morning, we headed out on Highway 11's gently sloping road on our way to Quetico Provincial Park. The Chippewa campground promised clean showers, power, and a beautiful lake to camp beside. Yet it was raining when we got there, forcing us to huddle under a tarp around the picnic table. Although the rain had stopped by morning, we had to pack up our gear wet. By this point, we're road-hardened enough that we didn't mind.

Life In A Time-Warp

We stopped for photos at the Atlantic watershed – the high point east of which water flows into the Atlantic Ocean.

As trivia goes, it seemed to us to be quite profound. This part of northern Ontario has a magical time-forgotten feel to it. Although the prosperity of the '50s and '60s road trip days are gone, this area still feels like you could disappear into here and no one would even notice. The sensation was never truer than at Sheri Turner's house near Shebandowan.

We didn't know Sheri, but she invited us to stay at her home on the recommendation of a Warmshowers host we had contacted in Thunder Bay – a person we had yet to meet. Sheri lives alone and does not have a home so much as her own little world, one she welcomed us into with ebullience and energy. Her immaculate property, called The Settlement – we pondered the many possible interpretations of the name – is a house and panoply of outbuildings, mostly painted grey with bold accents of red everywhere. It's part fantasyland, part museum and also, one imagines, part window into her soul. As we arrived, we found Sheri wrapping up a tour of 'her' woodlot for a couple of curious naturalists.

She doesn't own the land on which the woodlot sits, but she maintains it like a room in her house. The floor of the woodlot is so clear of debris it feels like carpeting that you could lay down and spend the night on. She explained that cleaning and straightening up is her obsession. It's one of the reasons why, although she's 60, she continues to clean rooms at the Timberline Motel, just a few kilometres down the road.

Sheri Turner

Sheri is an incurable sentimentalist and relentless collector; each of the hundreds of knickknacks in her house has a place and a history. In the bathroom, above the mirror I see a column of vintage tins that once held aspirin, salve and laxatives: In one bedroom is a collection of paraphernalia from relatives' service during the Second World War; in another, an original Hudson's Bay blanket and a tikinagan, a baby carrier Indigenous people used to safely dangle their infant on a tree. In other places, there's grandma's riding pants and books, a retro Coke bottle collection (although she doesn't drink the pop), quilts, family photos, and scrapbooks full of clippings about family events or local history. Over her red (naturally) fridge, her cookbooks are sorted by recipes that match holiday events, like Christmas and Easter.

She often finds herself absorbed in books about her family history, and explains she'll often stay up late into the night reading them. "I can't sleep because they're too interesting," she says.

Along with Sheri's skills as a sewer, quilter, and home decorator, she learned the skill of carpentry from her dad. After she bought the house in 2012, she added a dormer – yes, by herself – renovated the old garage, and then created the other buildings that accent the site. Those structures include a greenhouse, a wistful doll house with star lights on the ceiling for her five grandchildren, a comical outhouse with his-and-her seating, and a pergola that has a distinctly resort vacation feel.

As we tour the property, I video-record her describing how each building came about and what it means to her. I call the resulting video Sheri Turner's Enchanted World. She insisted that we sleep in her guestrooms. We woke up at 7 a.m. sharp to a knock on the door, announcing that breakfast was on the table.

It is nearly the end of July as we approached Thunder Bay, where we will begin the ride across the north shore of Lake Superior – a gruelling route many consider the most challenging of the cross-Canada trip. This day, there was more downhill than uphill and we made good time getting to the spectacular Kakabeka Falls and then on to Thunder Bay. There, we met Warmshowers host Frank Pollari in Fort William, the rougher working-class side of the city.

Allison in Frank's backyard commune.

Frank is a remarkable guy – although legally blind, he still rides his bicycle (accompanied by riders, who act as his guides). And he has an old Chrysler minivan that he invites his guests to drive. We hopped into the van and rode up to the top of Mount MacKay for an overview of the city and the Sleeping Giant rock formation in Lake Superior. Frank's house is a modest bungalow, but it was teeming with life. It's a true cyclists' commune, with a backyard full of tents. We met Gabriel from Quebec, Ian a solo cross-Canada rider who was about to give up his ride because of an inflamed knee, and Chaq, who was riding to raise awareness about abused children.

The next day, we drove Allison to the airport so that she could get back to start a new job in Calgary. But minutes later, we got an anxious call from her – WestJet has turned her away because her driver's licence was expired and therefore not accepted as ID. Allison was afraid that if she didn't get home quickly she might lose her new job. A frantic afternoon of phone calls later, we connected with the Alberta Motor Association, which issued a temporary licence so she could catch a flight the next day. While Allison fretted, the rest of us passed the afternoon at the Dawson Trail Craft Brewery. Just a half-block away is Bennett's

Bakery, home of the Persian, a doughnut-like pastry with a berry icing on top. It was created in the 1940s by Art Bennett, the bakery's founder. Bennett claimed that after John Joseph "Black Jack" Pershing, a U.S. Army General, visited his bakery Bennett decided to name his creation after him. It's a Thunder Bay thing, but after a tasting we concluded they are highly overrated.

The next day, we drove Frank's van to the Terry Fox Monument on the east end of town and then got Allison on her plane. Frank had gone out kayaking and camping overnight – leaving his home in the hands of his guests – and I headed out to pick him up at Jarvis Bay, about 45 minutes south. After an afternoon social at the Community Spokes bicycle cooperative, we headed back to Frank's for his weekly jam with local musicians. Such are the random magic moments of this trip. As Frank played harmonica in his living room, guitarists Dave, Mike and Fred took turns playing jazz, folk, and classic tunes to a jammed house. Do you know any J.J. Cale, I asked Dave. "Do I," he said. And the four launched into a rockin' tune.

Riding Into Danger

We traced our way north out of town along quiet streets the next morning, but the road soon turned threatening. Many cross-Canada cyclists consider the Trans-Canada Highway across the top of Lake Superior to be among the most scenic, most physically challenging and, in some cases, also the most dangerous. In particular, there are sections between Thunder Bay and Nipigon that feel like death traps.

One of them nearly ensnared me.

Much of the road between those two communities is two-lane and absent of shoulders for bicyclists to ride on. Cyclists are forced to balance on the white line at the edge of the road, hoping that passing motorists will give them respectful space. The shoulders are typically loose gravel that could send a bike out of control. Many of the bridges are even more dangerous – extremely narrow, with no room beyond the pavement. It's on one of these bridges that I had the biggest scare of our cross-Canada ride. As I approached a bridge, I saw oncoming traffic but carried on because there were no cars behind me. About the mid-point of the bridge, however, one of the oncoming cars pulled out to pass the traffic, even though there was a double line. I looked up and saw a dark red Charger in my lane coming right at me. Had there been a gravel shoulder, I would have taken it, but to my immediate right was a concrete curb leaving me nowhere to go.

The driver of that car must've seen me in my bright clothing waving frantically but, instead of pulling back in, he kept coming right at me. As I edged against the concrete curb, the Charger missed me by centimetres and within seconds was gone. Behind me, the other members of the ConnecTour team had seen the situation developing and waited to see my fate.

Once across the bridge, I stopped to let my racing pulse slow down and my anger subside. In my view, there are roads that are poorly designed but it's the drivers who make them dangerous roads. There is no way that driver should have been passing anyone on the bridge, and it is almost criminally irresponsible that he carried on when he saw me there. That evening, we agreed none of us would enter a narrow bridge if there is traffic coming from either direction.

The road ahead over the next week was filled with stunning scenery, wildlife and shuttered motels with broken down doors, plywood on the windows and graffiti on the tattered walls. What there isn't much of is camping. We stopped at a place called Canyon Country Co-op, because we were told it's bicycle friendly but the grounds were barren. We turned back a kilometre to Wolf Canyon, an unserviced campground where we met Eleanor who was riding her Honda 500 motorcycle to Winnipeg. The next day, we rode another 102 kilometres looking for anywhere to rough camp. Eventually we set up on a gravel road that runs beside Lower Nishi Lake, a half-kilometre off the highway. Erecting tree branches to divert wayward ATVs from our tents, we jumped into the warm lake to rinse away the day's sweat. The next day, we were enraptured by the morning mist hanging over Superior as we glided down a long descent to a waterfront picnic spot near Roswell.

A few kilometres east, in the town of Shreiber, we stopped at a convenience store. A disabled man who appeared to be in his early 20s named Morgan greeted us and told us his dad, Mark, runs the potato chip truck next door. COVID may have idled a lot of businesses, but Mark said the day before we arrived he sold 630 pounds of potatoes as fries. We needed potatoes because the convenience store didn't have them, and Mark handed us a bag.

An Historic Port Lost In Time

We rode the 105 km over hilly roads to Neys because there are private and provincial campgrounds there. Learning the provincial campground is full, we turned to the private campground. The host turned us away, telling us it was fully booked with seasonal workers. "Can we camp in that open area over there?" asked Rick. "Nope," said the owner. It was obvious to us that this host had a thing about cyclists. We were running out of options. The owner's wife, Tami, told us there's a ghost town just a few kilometres further east at Port Coldwell. Our eyes lit up with curiosity.

It is easy to miss the turnoff to Coldwell, and our initial impression was disappointment. Just across the railroad tracks was an eerie, overgrown cemetery that looked like it was straight out of a horror movie. We carried on down an overgrown trail towards the lake.

There we found the foundations of a few long-gone buildings, a rusted boiler, and a partially sunken ship across the bay. Yet the bay was stunning and utterly still. It was to become one of our favourite camping spots on the entire trip. Far from the noise of the highway, we set up on the edge of the water, looking at a bay that is sheltered by a massive rock outcrop. We later learned that

Canada's famous Group of Seven travelled to Port Coldwell in the 1920s, and Lawren Harris portrays the hamlet in a painting called "Coldwell Bay," Lake Superior, 1923.

Port Coldwell was once a fishing and shipping port. Before the decline of the Lake Superior fishery in the mid-20th century, its economy and way of life was sustained by commercial fishing. Long before there were roads, the railway that passed through Coldwell brought the fish catch to market.

Dave Sill, an Environment Canada scientist who lives in Barrie, Ont., has a close personal connection to the town. On the Info Superior blog (https://infosuperior.com/blog/), he wrote that his grandmother Agnes Jean Johnson grew up in Port Coldwell.

"She had such wonderful stories about the place, and as I looked into it more, not only were her stories shown to be true but there was even more to love about the place."

"Agnes told the story of her mother making pies for her to bring up to the artists painting from boxcars on the tracks up the hill ("Now don't bother them!"). These of course were the Group of Seven artists that produced stunning imagery of Coldwell, Pic Island, and Lake Superior. An A. Y. Jackson painting of Port Coldwell even shows the house where my grandmother grew up (see painting directly below; her house is bottom left). It still amazes me."

"Port Caldwell," by A.Y. Jackson.

Here are the lyrics to Dave's song:

Coldwell Bay (Dave Sills) © 2019

Train pulled in for water and some Nicoll Brothers trout
Hauled up past the ice house while the nets were drying out
Gid and Eileen Nicoll had the biggest house around
On the rocky north shore of Superior, in this lonely fishin' town

Well Gideon played the fiddle, Eileen she played guitar
For miners, teacher, loggers, preacher, and the Mountie from afar
And ol' one-armed Bert, the CPR clerk, and the painters from down south
They waltzed while the scent of Eileen's flowers drifted all around the house

Lake was cold, life was hard
But they danced the dark away

Saturdays at the Nicoll place
In a town on Coldwell Bay

The lamprey came, stole all the fish, shut the business down
Gid and Eileen, they met their fate on the tracks at the edge of town
Government men, they razed it all, gone without a trace
But every spring Eileen's flowers bloom all 'round the old Nicoll place.

Tracing Superior's Stark Grandeur

At this point in the ride, there were just three of us, Rick, Tanya and me, as we left our beautiful bay. We rode for a day-and-a-half on Highway 17, leaving the Superior shoreline at Marathon (birthplace of the real Winnie the Pooh) into an endless vista of boreal forest dotted with countless lakes. Only the occasional roar of passing trucks on the Trans-Canada kept us from lulling into a coma-like state. Stopping for lunch on Aug. 4 in White River, we considered our limited camping options on the road ahead. Rejecting one spot recommended on an app that identifies random campsites, we carried on to Obatanga Provincial Park, which sounded almost ideal.

Almost. Except it was closed.

In fact, we learned it had been idled for about 10 years – decommissioned by the Ontario government during one of its cost-cutting campaigns. Out of options late in the day, we lifted the bikes around the chained gate and rode into the haunting park with its overgrown foliage and weeds popping through the crumbling asphalt. It felt eerily post-apocalyptic, with abandoned campsites gradually being devoured by a multi-tentacled green monster. We rode deeper into the abyss until we found a former day use area near a small lake. A large playground set in bright reds and yellows and blues was not far from the laundry/shower building. Walking into the building, we found the washers and dryers abandoned and slowly turning to rust. The flush toilets in the adjacent washrooms were crammed with garbage and the plumbing long-since destroyed. We set up for the night near the playground and cooked a meal of chicken.

The next day, just as we had lifted our bikes back over the gate, a parks truck pulled up. The two workers seemed entirely disinterested in why we were there and didn't bother to ask us whether we had poached a stay. "What happened to this park?" I asked one of them. "I don't know," he said, with a disgusted shrug. "It was decision of the government of the day."

The road into Wawa was easy and gently rolling, and we arrived there mid-afternoon. After a quick lunch, we went searching for our host – a friend of a friend – who agreed to let us camp in his yard. We were scheduled to have a day's rest, and I was ready for it. Although Wawa is an unremarkable place, James Smedley's house is located on the edge of Lake Wawa, one of the most scenic spots in town. Unfortunately, James, who is a wildlife photographer, was away working when he arrived, and he had forgotten to mention to his daughter Islay that there would be visitors. So, when three filthy cyclists rolled into her yard with laden-down Surlys, Islay looked like she was considering a call to 911. An hour later, however, as we had explained the arrangements, Islay relaxed and opened up the house to us. After a shower and dinner cooked in a real kitchen, we were charmed as Islay sang folk songs to us with her dog Mila at her feet.

With an all-day rain the next day, we focused on catching up on emails, banking and blogs. As preventative maintenance, we switched out the chains on the bikes and then I headed off to Wawa's most famous landmark: Young's General Store.

Wawa: Forever Young's

There I chased down, Anita Young, the surviving half of the couple who took over the store in 1971. Bill Young founded what has become a Wawa institution way back in 1971 and brought Anita into the business, first as an employee and eventually spouse. As the store grew over the years, it expanded into a potpourri of souvenir T-shirts, fishing bait and lures, food, gifts, ice cream, a player piano and – its most famous feature – a pickle barrel where buyers could pick their own. (It is now relegated to behind-the-counter service because of COVID-19 precautions.)

The store's growth over the years is even more remarkable, considering one devastating setback that could have easily destroyed the couple's dreams. Eight years after the store opened, in April 1979, the family awoke to the barking of their family dog, Tonka. They discovered the store and their attached home were in flames. Despite the efforts of the Michipicoten volunteer firefighters, the wood-frame building quickly surrendered to the flames. Bill, Anita and their three sons narrowly escaped.

Anita Young

"The door frame was on fire as we got out," says Anita.

Anita says Bill was a bit of a risk-taker and had left the building underinsured, which made rebuilding unrealistic. "Bill didn't believe in a whole lot of insurance," says Anita. "We were pretty short."

Fortunately for the Youngs, the townspeople stepped forward. "They said to Bill, 'Have you got enough money to buy the lumber?'" says Anita. "'If you can buy the lumber, we'll build it.'" And so, a crew of volunteers from town not only rebuilt Young's General Store, but also made it bigger and better than it had been before.

"The women brought food. ... Everybody from town came with the saws and ladders and nailing guns," Anita said. "We'll always be grateful, and we'll support the town."

Yet, more heartbreak came in 1988 when Bill, a lifelong smoker, died of lung cancer. The town turned out once again to help keep the store operating, and today it still operates with Anita, 73, when I visited her during this tour, and two of her three sons, Jim and Allan. The front is scattered with a broad array of artifacts – mementoes to the days when Wawa was a boom mining town, including old gas pumps, an ancient outboard motor, a Coke dispenser and a wringer washer. Beside the store stands the original massive Canada goose statue that the town erected to attract motorists passing by on Highway 17. When the goose was replaced with a more modern version a few years ago, Anita bought the old one and had it moved to the store.

The town rallied once again a few years ago to save Henrietta, the store's stuffed moose, after it was confiscated by provincial conservation officers. Local folks started a yellow ribbon campaign demanding Henrietta's return, got politicians involved and finally prevailed two years later when the moose was returned. (As it wore out from tourist use, it was eventually replaced by a bull moose, but that too was put in storage during the pandemic.)

The community's support through the Young's family crises have left Anita fiercely loyal to her town. And she always remembers Bill's adventurous spirit and determination to succeed.

"If you try, you can do it. There were a lot of hard times, but we did it," she said. "Fifty years already, I don't know where time goes. I still think it's not real."

The next morning's goodbyes to Islay had the now-familiar

sense of melancholy we'd experienced with the new best friends we had made throughout the trip. Heading out under grey skies and blustery winds, we once again glimpsed Superior's grandeur at Michipicoten River before heading inland at the boundary to Lake Superior Provincial Park. By the end of the day, we reached Agawa Bay and found a beautiful campsite on the shore of Lake Superior, just a day-and-a-half out of Sault Ste. Marie. For the first time, we were getting a taste of Ontario's summer holiday season, and it brought back memories of my days as a kid exploring Lake Huron with my parents. Much as the ConnecTour team enjoyed the adventure of camping alone off the highway in random sites; the midsummer shores of Superior felt welcoming.

There were a few "dips" – remember Rick's term for hills? – on the road into the Sault but we savoured the ride. As soon as we could escape the highway, we snuck into the Sault via secondary roads. When we rolled into the home of Warmshowers hosts Meaghan Perrotta and Jack Lewin, we discovered the lawn was still soaked from the week's rains. No worries! We were glad to spread our drop sheets for a couple of nights. The next day, we wondered around the old canal district and explored Mill Square, the gentrified former site of St. Mary's Paper, which closed in 2011. The once-industrial district, with its red sandstone buildings, has been transformed into a cultural hub that houses artists, entrepreneurs, businesses, the Algoma Conservatory of Music and Algoma University Fine Arts department.

Jack, it turned out, worked at Velorution, a bike shop in Sault Ste. Marie. That evening, we rode out to the house of Andre Riopel, former owner of the bike shop. Andre is a local celeb in The

Soo. He is a physiotherapist who is also passionate about cycling and the development of non-motorized recreational trails. Early in his career, he worked in sports medicine for the Soo Greyhounds major junior hockey team, and later served with Canada's national cycling team leading up to the 1984 Summer Olympic Games. He opened Velorution in 2006 but sold it in 2014 to free up more time to pursue other interests. As director of the Sault Cycling Club Advocacy, he has been the linchpin for the development of a city-wide interconnected trail system. We borrowed some mountain bikes from him and headed out with Jack and Andrew to try out a few trails that were nearing completion. The rolling and treed trails were challenging for road cyclists who had grown accustomed to pavement but we laughed gleefully as we gingerly navigated our way through the woodlot north of town while experienced riders zipped by us. We rode until dark and had to make our way back to Jack and Meaghan's with lights on.

As we left the Sault, we headed east along the Great Lakes Waterfront Trail toward the home of another Warmshowers host. Canada's secondary roads are not only more peaceful and scenic to ride than the highways, but they also often lead to the serendipity that added to the richness of our experience. We were in Amish country, and it was to be another day of discovery. In the early 2000s, 20 Orthodox Mennonites (also known as Amish) families moved into the area, driven away from southern Ontario by the rising cost of farmland. These families are very traditional, with unadorned clothing and off-grid homes, yet they do not live in isolation. They interact with the broader community by providing services, such as building sheds, re-roofing, and selling cedar siding and cedar posts for fencing.

As we rode along Maple Ridge Road, we spotted a sign out front of one farm advertising fresh vegetables and eggs. Something about this sign convinced us it was the right place to stop and stock up for the day. When we pulled in, the horse-drawn buggies and traditional attire of the people there signalled we had arrived at an Amish farm.

We were greeted by Anna Stutzman, matriarch of the family, one of her daughters and a grandchild.

They seemed to delight in the novelty of watching us arrive on bicycles, rather than the air-conditioned SUVs that typically pull into the driveway. Ely and Anna Stutzman have owned this 160-acre farm since 2008, when they came with the Amish migration. Ely said the family moved from the Orillia area, drawn by the fertile and affordable land around Thessalon. They built their plain white two-storey clapboard house, all the outbuildings and then set to work tilling the land in the machine-free way that comes with Amish life. Working the land is incredibly labour-intensive; ploughing a field, for example, is done with two-furrow hand-guided ploughs pulled by a team of six horses. On a good day, the team will turn over three acres of soil.

"The fields are long, so we stop about every third of the distance to give the horses a rest," said Ely.

The homestead is no-frills and yet felt cozy as the family bustled about their daily chores. In accordance with their faith, the Stutzmans kept the house off the grid – there is no electricity to power indoor lights, only kerosene lanterns. Cooking and heating are mostly done with wood that is hand-cut and hauled to the house. A vegetable garden behind the house was bursting with broccoli, parsley, onions, garlic, beets and other produce that will be used by the family and sold to passersby. Nearby, a dozen hummingbirds swarmed around a feeder, zipping in and out of our group as we stood chatting. One of the barns had several carriages sitting out front.

"I'm a wagon-maker," said Ely. He makes and fixes the wagons and wheels for the entire community – a craft he hopes one of his sons will carry on (the couple also has four daughters). The iron-clad wooden wheels take a beating on these gravel roads, so Ely's skills are constantly in demand.

Ely also owns a sawmill and sells sawn cedar to a local supply company. On the next-door farm we could hear one of Ely and Anna's sons urging horses on, trying to pull a wagon overloaded with wood. Ely gave his head a disapproving shake as he watched his son shout at the horses. How many horses does the farm have, I asked. Ely looked bewildered, and then replied, "As many as I need." It took another minute of calculation before he reported he has 14 horses, and sometimes brings in a few more from the "outsiders" when the work justifies it.

The Amish uniform is straw hats for men, full beards and mustaches shaved off. As Ely doffed his hat, he revealed a bald head. Like his sons, he wears a deep blue buttoned-up shirt and plain jeans. Although the Amish are closely related to Mennonites, they follow their own path. The roots of the Amish faith go all the way back to 1693, when Jakab Ammann led a schism in the church. They are deeply committed to a simple way of life, Christian pacifism and a rigid resistance to modern technology. There are no iPhones here. They value rural life, the rewards of hard labour, humility and submission to what they believe is the will of God. They also do not believe in being photographed, because in their view personal photographs can call attention to one's self. I reluctantly agreed to Ely's polite request to put the camera away.

Many times, I have seen these people in their buggies and thought of them as something outside of society. My visit with the Stutzmans changed my view. They seem happy and fulfilled, and they make a valued contribution to our social mosaic. Although their practices are based in scripture, it also strikes me that they have simply chosen an alternative way of living. Here, a few kilometres outside of Thessalon, it doesn't feel like a bad choice at all.

We carried on into Thessalon via the Waterfront Trail and stopped for lunch at a park where the Thessalon River flows into Lake Huron. We struck up a chat with some local folks who were picnicking there. After a few minutes, one of the men who had been listening to our story with a baffled grimace, asked the question that must have tumbling around in his mind since he met us.

"How bored do you have to be to want to ride your bicycles across Canada?" he said.

Rick and I looked at each other in astonishment. It was time to leave.

A Video We Hope You Never See

That night, we rolled into the property of a Warmshowers

host known as Tome – which we later learned was meant to be "Tom E". His clapboard home was unpainted and the yard was scattered with metal debris and cars in various states of disrepair. Tom wasn't there when we arrived but we uncovered a garden hose under the overgrown grass. Tanya stripped down and hosed off, while Rick and I explored the property looking for an area safe to set up. A half-hour later, a car pulled into the driveway and a man who said he's a neighbour of Tom's had come to investigate who the heck were the intruders on his property. "Tom called me and asked me to check you out. He said he saw a naked woman on his security cam, showering with a hose."

Tom had forgotten we were coming. We laughed at the misunderstanding and then prayed the security cam footage wouldn't find its way to social media.

As the neighbour left, the sunny skies turned black and a fierce wind signalled a storm was imminent. We scrambled to erect our tents and I got mine up just as the skies broke open. I jumped inside and quickly realized that the vicious wind was threatening to overpower my hasty set-up. I laid on my back and braced the poles with my arms and legs as the winds tore at the nylon, and yet one pole still broke under the strain. I must've been in that position for a half-hour before the gale subsided and we were able to come out and assess the damage. Fortunately, it was nothing that couldn't be MacGyvered – our all-encompassing term for countless impromptu side-of-the-road repairs. In fact, Rick, with a resourcefulness borne from decades of experience, had packed a pole patch that had my tent looking reasonably fit until I had time to fix it properly.

Tom eventually returned home and apologized for sending the neighbour over. He explained he collects useful junk from the area landfill, where we works, and is even converting an old Prius to provide backup power for the house. In the morning, he brought freshly baked curried bread out to us to send us off in style.

Finding Family

The next day was to be a big one for me. We were planning to turn south at Spragge to cross Manitoulin Island on our way to southern Ontario, but first we would take a small side trip east to a hamlet called Nairn Centre, just west of Sudbury, so we could visit with my niece, Amy and her husband Ed Mazey. Although the couple grew up in southern Ontario, they had embraced the wilds surrounding Sudbury with enthusiasm. Amy knows how to skin a deer. They breed dogs and raise chickens. When we arrived, Amy proudly announced she had been certified as a volunteer firefighter (and after our visit, she was elected mayor). Ed is a lawyer for a large mining company based in Sudbury and leaves the outdoor adventures to Amy. My sister Lynne and her husband Norm Withers had also driven up from the Sarnia area to visit with us.

Doug's niece Amy, sister Lynne and brother-in-law Norm.

As expected, Ed and Amy were the perfect country hosts. We had a large meal with barbecued beef, potatoes, and three desserts - apple pie, ice cream and peaches. The only glitch was my overnight sleep in the basement. There's no bathroom down there – a major problem for those with enlarged prostates – and when I headed upstairs in the middle of the night, I discovered the door to the main floor was locked. Fortunately, I found the basement workshop had access to the exterior. I was once again peeing in the wild!

In this part of Ontario, Warmshowers hosts get a bit scarce but Amy and Ed knew a couple through their church who were willing to let us camp the next night. Their home on Manitoulin Island was just nine kilometres from the Chi-Cheemaun, the ferry that would take us to Tobermory the next day. We left Nairn Centre at about 7:30 and rode steadily through rolling territory until we crossed the bridge to Manitoulin Island and stopped for lunch at the Manitoulin Brewing Company. It was a 130-kilometre day, and it was nearly 5 p.m. by the time we pedalled up Ed and Shirley's driveway. Their upgraded century home sits perhaps 200 metres off the highway, cuddled by mature trees. Ducks wandered through the yard. With COVID still on a rampage, we agreed we would wear masks when we entered the house and keep contact to a minimum. Shirley made us muffins and shared lentil-and-chicken soup with us, just like we were old friends. In less than 12 hours with them, that's how we felt.

It was now mid-August, and the bloom of summer was developing little brown edges. This day, I was feeling excited, anxious and almost tearful because we planned to rendezvous with Lisa in Tobermory – the first time we would have seen her in person since the crash in Saskatchewan on July 5. Lisa had been staying with her mom in Windsor while she waited for her broken collarbone to fuse back together. Increasingly restive, she decided she would buy a van and come meet us, effectively being our support vehicle until she was well enough to resume cycling. The ferry ride from South Baymouth to Tobermory was magical, with sunny skies and a strong headwind ripping at our hats and clothes. We found Lisa parked downtown, and I broke into tears as we embraced. In the back of her van was her Surly bike and gear. I had no doubt that she would be back on the ride as soon as her body would allow her.

Reuniting with Lisa had a surrealistic quality to it. After her dangerous crash, it felt as though she had effectively been lost to me, and to the group. Then one day she just miraculously reappeared.

9. SOUTHERN ONTARIO

A LONG-AWAITED REUNION

We left Bruce Peninsula National Park, where we camped for the night, and headed for Lion's Head, a sleepy tourist town halfway down the Bruce Peninsula. I had only been to Lion's Head once before in my life – more than six decades ago when I was about 3 – and yet I have vague memories of old wooden cabins close to the Georgian Bay beachfront. The cabins are gone now, and the village is full of tourists but there is something still very familiar about its feel. We camped at the waterfront municipal park.

The next day, on the road to Wiarton, we were travelling down Route 9, a quiet secondary road when we came across a man with a painter's easel by the side of the road, capturing a dilapidated house that sat rotting in a nearby field.

Giving in to my curiosity, I stopped and discovered he was Greg Bailey, an animator who produced 20 years of episodes for the Arthur kids animated series for PBS. He paints as a hobby. We left him and rolled on into Wiarton, had lunch by the statue to Wiarton Willie, the mythical groundhog who forecasts spring, and then headed west to a Warmshowers host's home on Sauble Bay, near the sandy shore of Lake Huron. We swam and bathed in the warm, shallow bay. Our next day's destination, in Owen Sound, was to be a rest day. We had rented a couple of rooms at a grand old mansion called the Eddie Sargent House, a glorious old home with its third-storey observation tower. Built by a general merchant in 1887, the house was eventually bought by Sargent, who was the town's mayor before he served in the Ontario legislature as a Liberal MPP from 1963 to 1987. After he died in 1998, his family sold the stately old home. Today, it is owned by Sim Salata, curator at the Grey Roots Museum & Archives. She takes in guests to help offset the cost of maintaining the home. My oldest daughter, Carla, her husband Kevin, and their three boys came up to visit us.

Now safely past the wilds of northern Ontario, our ranks grew again. Lynn Marshall, a fellow Albertan, rejoined us with plans to go all the way to St. John's. Doug Reid, an Ontarian who had been following us on Strava, joined us for a couple of weeks. Counting Lisa in the van, we were back up to six travellers.

The next day, the ConnecTour group stopped to visit Tom Maloney, a long-time newspaper colleague, now retired, and his wife Wendy before heading to our next Warmshowers host just east of Thornbury. Then on to Phelpston, where we spotted an historic old bar that was announcing its reopening. We learned that owners Kim Sandy and Roy Cooper reopened the facility the very day we stopped there – Aug. 20, 2021 – after it was closed during Covid. The establishment had fallen on hard times during previous entities as a strip bar and biker bar, but Kim and Roy have just completed a family friendly reno. As we cycled through the bucolic farmland, I thought of how much this part of Ontario reminded me of my youth on a farm in southwestern Ontario. Decrepit barns in faded grey wood dotted the landscape. Old broken-down ploughs and rakes sat rusting in fields of weeds. Modern farm equipment, including massive tractors, were in almost every driveway.

Our evening near the hamlet of Coldwater would prove to be one of our most memorable of the entire trip. Our Warmshowers hosts, Marion Tilstra and Manda Freyman, cooked up a perfect stew for tired cyclists – a magical home and equally welcoming spirit. Manda, who now runs a fitness business, is an intense cyclist who started an all-female mountain bike ride group called Peace and Wheelies a few years ago. Her partner Marion is an OPP officer.

Marion & Manda

The couple has a home in a rural wooded area near the hamlet. Located inland from the base of Georgian Bay, it is literally about as middle-of-nowhere as you can get in southern Ontario. Their home is a renovated cottage adorned in front with white and yellow daisies. The back of the house feels like a sanctuary, with a sprawling deck complete with outdoor shower, rambling wooded yard, workout cabin, and firepit custom-designed with a bike-themed iron grate. We instantly bonded over our common love of cycling and stayed up late sharing stories over a roaring fire in the backyard. By morning as we reluctantly said our thank yous and goodbyes, Rick and I chuckled to each other – we could have just stopped the trip right then and stayed there indefinitely.

But, of course, we could not. We were on a mission with thousands of kilometres yet to go.

That morning, we said goodbye to Doug Reid, who was heading home in Listowel. The next couple of days, we slogged through pretty and gently rolling countryside, camping at unremarkable campsites. With Lisa as our unofficial support vehicle, we were able to offload some of our heavy gear and felt the freedom that comes with a lighter ride. Lisa, unfortunately, was getting bored with being our advance person and anxious to get back on two wheels. Yet her confidence was as shaky as her collarbone was weak. It was too soon for her. Three days from our Utopia in Coldwater, we muscled through undulating roads leading into Bancroft. Our Warmshowers hosts, Greg Cooper and Carolyn Brown, owned a sprawling home a few kilometres out of town on Bay Lake. With Greg away, Carolyn assumed full hosting duties. Within minutes, we were in swimsuits doing cannonballs off the dock into the refreshing lake. No need to set up your tents, Carolyn assured us – there was plenty of room in a guest house above the garage.

Carolyn is a doctor with privileges at the local hospital. As Lisa discussed her collarbone with Carolyn, wondering when she might be able to ride again, the doctor told us she would see if there were any open timeslots for an X-ray that evening. Less than two hours later, Carolyn had the results and told Lisa it appeared the bone had fused. With caution and careful exercise, Lisa could resume riding within perhaps a couple of weeks. We raised our glasses in celebration, not only to the good news but also to the kindness of this person who just two or three hours earlier had been a total stranger.

Bay Lake feels like a lover you have grown old with. It is not fresh and new, but its age has seasoned it into something irresistible. It takes one back to carefree days in cottage country; its still waters inviting the dip of a paddle. It forgives and gives. It is, at once, in this moment and in moments from decades past. It is another place where you can drop anchor for a day or a week or summer or perhaps forever.

But we didn't do that. We left in the morning on a day that would turn out to be one of craziest of our trip.

It was one of those days when I started the morning with an earworm: You're Only Human by Raggin' Boneman. Our plan was to cycle from Bancroft to a hamlet called Cloyne. The paved directions were Route 63 south to Highway 7 and then back up Route 41 to the hamlet. It was an inconvenient U-shaped route. Rick, our navigator, spotted an alternative that could save us perhaps 50 kilometres of riding. There was a logging road that cut across the U and would keep us away from busy Highway 7. After being run off the road by a logging truck that morning, I was ready to try anything that would get us away from traffic.

Shortcut To Hell

By this point in our ride, Rick had earned the nickname Shortcut. With his GPS-enabled phone mounted on his handlebar, he would often make course changes on the fly. Sometimes, they were fortuitous; sometimes they were dead ends.

And then, there was the shortcut to Cloyne.

Turning off the paved Route 63, I felt a sense of dread as we encountered gravel the size of golf balls, deep potholes, loose sand and several small hills. I turned to co-rider Lynn and said, "It had better not be like this the whole way." Within a half-hour of bone-jarring bumps in intense afternoon heat, Lynn declared she was out; she would cycle back and take the long way around. We briefly considered asking Lisa to bring the van down the gravel road to pick Lynn up, but the road was so rough we felt there was a good chance the vehicle would get trashed on the way. Instead, Lisa would drive around the paved route and find Lynn where we entered the shortcut.

Meanwhile, Rick, Tanya and I carried on along the gravel road, our arms numb from the constant jarring and our asses out of the saddle as much as possible to ease the battering of our spines. It was hot, humid and buggy. For the only time during our trip, I took my sweaty helmet off because it was constantly wobbling into my face. We kept moving to keep the bugs at bay. We powered our way up hills and then raced down the other side, risking crashes in the sandy ruts at the bottom to keep momentum for the next climb. It was the longest shortcut I'd ever known, and I began to believe that the 50 K extra distance on the pavement would have likely been faster.

Then things got worse.

Perhaps two-thirds of the way through the route, I was ahead of the other two riders. I came across a car stopped in front of me, and an excavator digging up the road up ahead. "Looks like we won't get through today," said the driver of the car. I felt a sudden flash of anger and said, "We'll see about that." I rode up to the excavator and saw that he was digging out a culvert, with about a metre of roadway left untouched. "Do you mind waiting until I and my friends get through?" I asked.

"Go ahead," said worker. But as I rode on, I heard, "But you won't make it through the next one."

Sure enough, another half-hour down the road, I came across another excavator and this time the entire road had been dug up. We were essentially trapped – no way forward and no avenue of retreat. I rode up to the excavator and asked him how long the project would take. I thought it might be a multi-day project. "Give us an hour," he said.

Rick, Tanya and I took advantage of the delay to have a prolonged lunch and dip in a beautiful lake near the road. Within the hour, the new culvert had been installed and we were able to carry on. Yet it was still another hour of hard riding before we made it back to pavement. I laughed at the absurdity of the experience, and in my mind decided Rick would forever be known as Shortcut.

We had lost Doug Reid, but the day after the shortcut from Hell, we were joined by Andy Williamson, a long-time friend of Rick and Tanya's who had recently retired and moved from Calgary to a home he had built at Christie Lake, near Perth. Andy had a disastrous day reaching us. When he set out from home, he didn't get far before he blew a tire and crashed his bike. He went home, found a replacement tire and set out again, only to have a second flat, although thankfully not a second crash. But as he set out the third time, a bird dive-bombed him, with droppings down his shirt and even through the vents in his helmet. When he phoned Rick to update him, the sun was setting and Andy still was still 30 kilometres away from us. Rick dashed off in the van to rescue Andy.

Another earworm creeped into my head: I Feel Good, by James Brown.

The next morning Andy guided us to the home he shared with his partner Krystyna on Christie Lake. Its tranquillity reminded me of Bay Lake, but on a grander scale. Andy and Krystyna's house has massive windows that provide a panoramic view of the bucolic lake. After dinner, Andy took me out to his music studio in the garage. Before a successful career in engineering, Andy had been the drummer in a band called Big Bang Theory (long, Andy noted, before the TV show of the same name). They were almost famous, with some radio airplay and even a few videos on Canada's Much Music television channel, but the big break never came, and Andy chose to pursue a career with more economic certainty.

Brent McLaren

Now retired, Andy wanted to return to his first love, working as a studio musician and perhaps drumming for bands as needed. In the garage, he put on the music to Rush's YYZ, and played a note-for-note performance of the work done by Rush's great drummer Neil Peart.

We took the next day off and drove into Perth where Andy had arranged a personal tour of downtown with Brent McLaren, the amiable and animated Perth Town Crier. With his bushy white beard, wireframe glasses and generous girth, he looked like Santa on summer break. Over the next couple of hours, as we wandered around the historic canals, unusually wide streets, and immaculately maintained brick and stone buildings, McLaren gave us a thorough briefing on the charming little town, which was founded in 1816 – ancient by the standards of us prairie dwellers. We learned about Matheson House, built for Roderick Matheson who was, according to our tour guide, almost universally despised in town because he controlled every aspect of the local economy. After fighting in the War of 1812, Matheson moved to Perth in 1817 where he married twice and fathered 11 kids, plus, legend suggests, a couple more.

By 1840, he opened Shaw & Matheson – claimed to be the first department store in North America. In later years, Matheson became a politician and a Conservative member of the Senate of Canada from Confederation in 1867 until his death six years later. At the former Gerdworth's drug store, we learned that back in the day you could get a whiskey prescription there.

In fact, Perth residents were so enamoured of liquor the town is reputed to be the birthplace of the mickey bottle – notwithstanding the prominence of Presbyterian churches, the congregants of whom, McLaren told us, just couldn't get along. Many of the homes were built with Potsdam Sandstone, and St. James Garrison Church (1819) was built using construction techniques that were later used in Canada's Parliament buildings. We wrapped up the tour by visiting the memorial to the Mammoth Cheese. The 10,000-kilogram mountain of cheese was produced from the milk of 10,000 cows in the Perth area in 1893 and shipped to Chicago for the World's Columbian Exposition to promote Canadian cheese around the world. It was two metres high and four metres in circumference and was so heavy it crashed through a floor while it was being delivered.

Perthians remain proud of it even now, nearly a century-and-a-half later.

After we finished the tour, we wandered around downtown and Lisa happened upon a fascinating local artist. She wrote this blog.

SEPTEMBER 3, 2021 / ONTARIO / BY LISA MONFORTON

Walking through the burnished wooden doors of Katherine Muir Miller's gallery on the main Street of Perth, Ont., is like walking into a delightful cross-section of Canada's natural beauty, painted impressionist in style, in lush and vivid colours.

Muir Miller's large landscape oil paintings draw you into iconic places, like British Columbia's majestic Mount Robson, Alberta's Moraine Lake or Quebec's Gatineau Hills. She is inspired by the beautiful places she's travelled in Canada, working from photographs she takes.

But how she arrived at this place, owning a gallery that showcases her artwork, with her beloved 11-year-old dog, Meeko, always at her side, has been a long, tough journey. During that time, she was forced to make choices in the face of pain and a sudden life change.

Six years ago, Muir Miller, 59, a mother of five who lives in Ottawa, was working as an emergency room nurse. But a traumatic fall from a height, in which she broke bones in her face and tore every muscle in the C2 area of her neck, forced her to give up her career and her athletic lifestyle. Before the fall, she played hockey on two women's teams, took ski trips every year to places like Banff, Lake Louise and Whistler, and had done a couple of triathlons. She was also the medical director of a kids' canoe camp in Temagami, Ont.

"I was super strong and didn't break my neck," says Miller. Talking

about the accident is still difficult.

Before the accident occurred, she had only dabbled in painting. But then, she began taking lessons with retired art teacher Gordon Harrison, an oil painter in Ottawa and several other artists. She signed up for an art retreat with Harrison early in her recovery.

"I went to the art retreat ... in a neck brace."

The first time she painted, she copied a work of Harrison's and said to herself, 'Did I just paint that?'

"I was now addicted to painting. I was like a sponge," says Muir Miller. As a perfectionist she tossed many of her early paintings in the trash, but she knew her newfound passion was helping her heal psychologically and emotionally.

"Those first couple of years, painting was an outlet for me; my hockey games went into that. I was like a crazy painter."

She said the process of painting prevented her from "spiralling into depression."

The more she painted, she more obsessed she became with making colours.

"You have to visualize to make colours. I was obsessed with 'how do I get that green?' I realized, I just needed practice."

She continued to paint at a ferocious pace, continually improving. Her husband, Fraser, told her that her paintings were looking stronger.

As she accumulated work, she began to do juried art shows for a few years but found them exhausting. Eventually, she began getting her work into galleries, such as the Santini Gallery in Ottawa. She also wanted to show in galleries in Montreal, where she was born and raised, as well as Muskoka and Toronto.

Then COVID hit. She was walking down Perth's shopping area on Gore Street with a friend when they spotted a store for sale at a reduced price. Her friend said she should consider opening a gallery here. With her husband's nudging and her friend, Darlene Kelly's business acumen – she had the vision that this is what she should do.

Muir Miller said the decision to make such a huge life change wasn't easy but was necessary.

"You have a head injury and are limited...you're not the same person. I could have gone on the road of self-pity and any medication I wanted."

But she chose to pursue her art instead. You can view her work at katherinemuirmiller.com.

That evening, a neighbour took us around Christie Lake on a pontoon boat to see some of the historic sites there. Of particular note was the "cottage" – actually a large home – owned by the Marks Brothers Dramatic Company, a group I frankly had no previous knowledge of. I later learned that over a 50-year period starting in the 1870s, the Marks Brothers Dramatic Company, composed of seven brothers and their wives, toured much of North America, playing to an accumulated audience of more than eight million people. In 1950, Maclean's magazine named the group Canada's "Entertainers of the half-century."

Between big cheese, hated business tycoons and an accomplished performance group, we concluded that during its long-past heyday, this little town consistently punched above its weight. Today, it is a treasure chest of memories that reach well back before Canada was a nation.

As the sun crept down into the trees, Lisa and Tanya slipped off the boat and swam in the lake. It was late August, and the late-day shadows were starting to stretch. We wanted to savour every minute of it.

It is a quick and direct 100 kilometres into Ottawa, even on the secondary roads. Lisa decided it was time to try riding. She drove ahead in the van, parked it and hopped on her unloaded bike to circle back and meet us. An hour later, as we huddled under a tree seeking shelter from a steady drizzle, we spotted her ripping past our rest stop. Although her Surly was not yet laden with gear, she was clearly ready to ride.

Our Warmshowers hosts that night, Richard (Guy) Briggs and Carole Sauvé, lived in the Centre-Ville district, beside the Ottawa River. They were as welcoming as their lives were out of the ordinary. Over the course of the evening, Richard told us how he learned to live without a car – a practice that continues even though they are now a family of four.

When he was in his early 20s, Richard offered to buy a Ford Fairmont that his father had decided to get rid of. But his father refused to sell it to his son, Briggs recalls, "Because you don't need a car." It was a lesson that Richard internalized so much that when his father offered to sell Richard a used Jetta a decade later, his son had concluded he didn't need a car at all. It was a remarkable decision for a family raising two kids in Ottawa, where winter temperatures can dip as low as -25 C.

But being without a car doesn't mean they were without wheels. In fact, the family gets much of its mobility from Richard's garage full of eclectic bicycles. Those two- and three-wheeled human-powered machines range from fairly conventional all-purpose bikes to tricycle recumbents, and a variety of Frankenbikes, with frames stretched into freakish designs. His collection includes cargo bikes, a "hammer head", chopper bikes – with unnaturally long front forks that look like the motorcycles of the same design – and one of his prized possessions – an authentic rickshaw that came back with the family from India after Carole returned from a diplomatic mission she served there. Carole, who works for Immigration Canada, has also served in Nairobi, Kampala, Beirut and New Delhi. Richard is also an international traveller, having cycled in Australia, New Zealand, Fiji, and the Cook Islands. After they were married, the couple spent their honeymoon cycling across Cuba.

Out of all his bikes, Richard seems to favour the custom-made three-wheel recumbent which can be expanded into a tandem to accommodate two riders. He's gotten innovative with that machine, adding bars so that it can carry a canoe or even lumber. He also attaches a home-made 4x8-foot trailer to it and has towed a Hammond organ through a parade. He has fitted many of his bikes with hub-based generators and flashing headlights and taillights. I'm delighted to learn he plans to ride with us on his recumbent bicycle for a couple of days, as we venture into Quebec.

Our relaxing dinner could not have foretold the dramatic night that awaited our overnight campout in Richard and Carole's backyard. At around 1:30 a.m., Lynn was awakened by someone apparently sneaking into the backyard. Fearing the person was trying to steal some of the team's expensive touring bicycles, she confronted the intruder aggressively, threatening him and shouting at him to leave.

"I lost it on him. I started screaming at him,'" Lynn said the next day. "And then he said, 'But I live here.'" It was Richard's son, Nico, who was coming home from his shift at a local bar.

Lynn crawled back into her sleeping bag, still shaking from the unexpected disturbance only to discover a few minutes later that someone was trying to get into her tent. "And I just started screaming. I just had so much adrenaline in me from the episode that happened 10 minutes before." This time, everyone was awakened to Lynn screaming, "Get out of here! Get out of here!" It turns out the intruder was Andy, who had gotten up a few minutes earlier for a bathroom break, had hit his head on a fence post and was temporarily disoriented. "I thought he wanted me," said Lynn with a laugh. "Then he came to his senses." Lisa and I cuddled in our tent and giggled for an hour.

Richard joined us the next morning as we headed out in steady rain, telling ourselves it would pass quickly. It didn't, and the first hour became tense as we struggled to maintain visibility and stay upright under an increasingly intense downpour. There were now seven of us in the group: Rick, Tanya, Lynn, Andy,

Richard and me, plus Richard's friend who was joining us for a couple of hours. Lisa was driving the van. Yet we were undeterred by the rain and more than ever driven to forge ahead. Somewhere in northern Ontario, we realized we had travelled more than half the distance across Canada, and now we were about to enter our final five provinces.

It might have been the moment I admitted to myself that – barring another Saskatchewan-size disaster – we truly were going to make the finish line.

10. QUEBEC

SEPTEMBRE EST SI BEAU

We rode through the rain on the relatively quiet Rte. Regionale 174 until we reached Cumberland, where we would take the ferry across the Ottawa River to Quebec. Although the rain was slowly easing, my bike slid on the wet metal ramp leading onto the ferry, making me fall onto my overstuffed panniers. I wondered how many times those bags had saved me from injury.

But it wasn't my riding that I was worried about – it was Richard's.

Riding with him was at turns interesting and terrifying. He seemed to be one of those daredevils who consistently tempted fate and came up smiling, time and again. That is, except for an incident he told us about that happened three years before we met him. Riding one of his freakish "tall" bikes, he fell, breaking his pelvis – requiring surgery. "Carole told me not to ride a tall bike again," he said with a chuckle. It was advice he chose to ignore.

As we ambled beside the pretty Ottawa River on Rte. 148, Richard often let his trike drift into the full lane with no apparent concern about the drivers coming up from behind. Remarkably, those drivers always saw him and gave him the space he had staked out. Yet by lunch, a couple of our group members were so agitated by his riding style, Rick was commissioned to give Richard a safety lecture. Richard reacted defensively, declaring that of the nine accidents he had been in over the years, he hadn't caused one of them. The afternoon ride to Montebello was unusually quiet.

But the tension lifted as we rolled into the yard of our Warmshowers host Michel Mailhot. I admit to having been a little anxious about how a group of English-speaking mostly western Canadians would be received in Quebec. Yet from the moment we met Michel until we left the province two weeks later, the welcome could not have been warmer and the people kinder. Assembling in his kitchen that evening, Michel picked up the fiddle and played us Quebec folk songs. That night, at his insistence, we slept in his bedrooms – mercifully spared from having to set up our rain-soaked tents.

There's a sleepy quality to the Ottawa River as it widens on its approach to the St. Lawrence. The current slows and the Ontario shoreline moves further away. At Carillon Canal

National Historic site and the adjacent hydro-electric facility, we stopped to survey Canada's tallest lock – where boats are raised and lowered 20 metres. Drifting on through Oka, we went past dozens of cannabis shops with large banners claiming to have the best prices in town.

We camped for the night at Parc national d'Oka, a provincially run park located where the Ottawa River meets the Lake of Two Mountains. Tomorrow, we will say goodbye to Richard, who is cycling back to Ottawa, and ride into Montréal to begin a weeklong break while Rick and Tanya fly to a family event in Colorado. Lisa and I decided it was time to see whether she was finally ready to park the van and get back on a fully loaded touring bike.

Lisa cycled into Montréal on its dedicated bike paths the next morning while I drove ahead with the van to meet the group before they dispersed for a week. Lisa and I had a day to return to some of our favourite spots in the city, having a Montréal bagel lunch and a leisurely evening.

The next morning, we loaded our bikes in the van and headed an hour north of Montréal to Saint-Jérôme, where we would test Lisa readiness to propel a fully loaded bicycle. The test would by conducted on Le P'tite Train du Nord, a 200-kilometre rail trail that stretches north to Mont-Laurier. The southern leg of the route was thick with day-trippers, and we covered just 35 kilometres before we broke for the day at the charming Auberge de la Gare. Lisa was in good spirits but tired. We found a great little patisserie down the road for dinner and crashed for the night. The next day, we rode another 35 kilometres to Saint-Faustin-Lac-Carre, and by the third day stretched the distance to 88 kilometres. Lisa's confidence and stamina were growing by the day, as we cruised through Mont Tremblant and the increasingly pastoral scenery under a gentle sun on our way to Nominingue, where we camped at a trail-side campground.

It was raining when we awoke, and we quickly packed up during a lull. We spotted Le Petit Cafe du Nord nearby. When we walked in, owner Carole Williams told us the café was not yet open for the day. "Could we just grab a pastry?" I asked. Before we knew it, the coffee was brewing. Carole told us she had bought the café a year before as a "retirement project." Sadly, with Covid, staff shortages were forcing her to restrict hours and making her put in 15-hour workdays.

Carole Williams

With a weary smile, she said that was never the plan. Thanking her for her hospitality, we headed out in a drizzle to the trail's northern terminus at Mont-Laurier. We were to stay in the Gîte au Pied du Courant, a bed-and-breakfast operated by a local artist. It turns out, the artist was the extraordinary Gilbert Desjardins. As he slowly relaxed with his new guests, he told us how a lifelong passion for African culture had led him to fill his home with remarkable artwork, wood carvings and ceremonial masks.

As a young man in the 1960s, Desjardins became interested

in the countries of Africa, including Sudan, Kenya, Senegal, Nairobi, Nigeria and Botswana. He also visited Rwanda several times from 1965 to 1969, decades before the brutal mid-1990s conflicts between Hutu and Tutsi in the former Belgian colony. Even then, he said, he saw evidence of genocide, "But there were no media there."

Gilbert Desjardins

Desjardins was deeply interested in being integrated into local tribes – learning their customs and understanding how modern influences are affecting them. "I prefer staying with these kinds of people," he said. To win acceptance into a tribe, he would set up camp within sight of a village for two or three days. Then, he would offer to help the women of the village with tasks like gardening while the men were off herding. Eventually, as he won their trust, they would invite him to come stay.

Over the years, pollution and climate change were having an increasing impact on these villages. As the desert spread, many tribes lost their ability to grow crops and were forced to migrate. Plastic pollution, meanwhile, was "everywhere on the coast, everywhere plastic," he said. "All the water bottles. Where there are many tourists, they just throw them away."

Desjardins set out to record these changes through his art. He photographs members of the tribe, often in beautiful traditional garb, and then digitally transforms the images into large, and often dark, canvasses that he enhances with acrylic paints. His work conveys the message that these Africans have been forced into climate migrations. His work is frequently exhibited in and around the Montréal-to-Mont-Laurier region. And it fills his beautiful riverside home on the banks of the Rivière du Lièvre. His home is also peppered with ceremonial masks bought from artists in Nigeria, a tall wooden giraffe he found in Nairobi, furniture and other wood carvings gathered from decades of world travel. In those other parts of the world, he has found similar effects from pollution. He told the story of visiting an island in New Guinea in 2008, where there was so much plastic the residents tried to migrate to another island. The residents on that second island turned them away.

Although he is in his 70s, Desjardin has no intention of slowing down his travels. In fact, he says, he likes this time of his life more than any other. He continues to work and run his gîte in the summer tourist season while planning trips back to Africa every winter.

I told him his home feels like a small paradise. “Yes,” he said. “But in winter, it is a prison.”

Perhaps in those endless grey days of January, that is true. It doesn’t feel that way now.

Un Petit Pas, Un Bond De Géant

Our trip on Le P'tite Train du Nord was not only a welcome break from our cross-Canada mission, but it also proved Lisa had healed enough to resume the bike ride. It was but a speck in our total distance but it bridged the ocean of post-traumatic doubts Lisa had been wrestling with since her crash. Soon, she would give up her van and start pedaling full-time. From Montréal, Lisa and I reconnected with our friends and then headed east on Sept. 7 along Rte. 138, tracing the St. Lawrence River. The ConnecTour team now consisted of Rick, Andy, Lisa, me and Colleen Ponzini, who had just joined. Earlier in the week, Lynn had struck out on her own, a bold decision for a petite and directionally challenged rider that not only worried the rest of us but also put us in the awkward position of not telling her husband Grizz – who fretted back home in Alberta – exactly what she was up to.

But there were more short-term concrete problems to contend with.

As I mounted my Surly in the Montréal suburb of Repentigny, I discovered the bottom bracket – the main bearing in the crank – had succumbed to countless turns and shattered to the point that my pedals flopped with every turn. Through incredibly good fortune, we discovered there was a bike shop just 500 metres from the park we were lunching at. Rick and I walked into Au Coin Du Pédaleur et du Coureur. We had previously been warned that the reception for 'les maudits anglais' can be a bit frosty in Quebec. Not here. "Oui," they have the part and "oui" we could use their tools. Within 20 minutes, we were back on the road.

That day, we rode to a small campground/RV park on the St. Lawrence called Chez Denise near the village of Lanoraie. Walking down to the beach that evening, we ran into a long-term camper who said his name in English was Raymond. We told him about the people we had met along the way, and reflected on how – even though every region we visited was distinct – there was something very Canadian about every one of those people.

> *"We're all Canadians," Raymond replied, looking out over the river. "And we're all human. We come from the same star. Some people forget that."*

Quebec is known as one of the most bicycle-friendly provinces in Canada. Much of the reason for that is the extensive Le Route Verte – Green Route – 5,300 kilometres of paths and roads throughout the province that put cycling in the forefront. Our trip along the St. Lawrence shoreline was just one part of that dreamy web. A series of easily spottable signs constantly diverted us away from the busy roads onto quiet streets rambling through bucolic Quebecois villages where cars were few and bikes were, if not royalty, as least given preferred status.

But even in ideal circumstances, drama was never far away. Riding east of Lanoraie in a steady rain, we found ourselves on a dangerous stretch of road in which the painted lines had sunk into the pavement a few centimetres over several years. The chubby 1.75 tires on our Surlys handled the hazard, but Andy was riding a speed bike with skinny tires. As we humped with our heads down to avoid the rain pelting on our faces, I heard Andy shout behind me as he went down. Turning around, I found him by the side of the road clutching his knee and grimacing in pain. There was nothing nearby, except a farmhouse at an intersection we had passed half-a-kilometre or so back. We headed there and found a mechanic working on a motorcycle in his garage. He didn't speak a word of English but we pointed to Andy's knee and convinced him to let us sopping wet cyclists into the warm, dry space to treat the wound. As we pulled out the medical kit, swabbed and patched, the mechanic turned his attention back to his Harley, looking back every few minutes to see how we were doing. Within a half-hour, Andy was patched up enough to continue and we were back on the road.

Over the next couple of days, we stopped at the stunning Sanctuaire Notre-Dame-Du-Cap in Trois-Rivières. Built at the site established as a chapel more than 300 years ago, it is ranked by the Catholic church as a minor basilica. The modern building, completed in 1964, is the second largest and most important Marian sanctuary dedicated to the Virgin Mary in North America after that of Our Lady of Guadalupe in Mexico. Even to non-Catholics, touring the imposing structure strikes awe and reverence. We rode through Trois-Rivières and found our Warmshowers host Benoit Caron, who had turned his cabin outside of town over to the ConnecTour crew. He had lived there while he built a large and modern permanent home on the same property. The next day, we continued on quiet back roads to Portneuf Natural Regional Park, and eventually Quebec City.

Pausing To Mark 9/11

On this, the anniversary, we paused to consider the significance of the day. It had been 20 years since the devastating terrorist attack on the World Trade Center in New York City. So much had changed and yet the social order the extremists had set out to destroy had carried on – albeit with significant inconveniences at airports and borders. We learned we could advance vote in the upcoming federal election, so we took the time to find a federal office, and then ambled over le Vieux Quebec and the Chateau Frontenac area. We spent much of the afternoon exploring the British fort and the Plains of Abraham. The date was also just two days short of the fateful day in 1759 when the British Army surprised the French in what would prove to be the turning point in the Seven Years' War over the fate of New France.

Lisa on the Plains of Abraham

We crossed the St. Lawrence to Levi the next morning. Lisa reluctantly took the wheel of the van while the rest of us got to savour a rare tailwind that allowed us to fly along at 30 km/h all day long. Le Route Verte took us through small towns with streets so narrow houses were practically on the road. The water along the shoreline was turbid and muddy from the stiff breezes, and the swaying reeds evoked an end-of-summer zeitgeist. We stopped that night at a roadside campground in Saint-Jean-de-Port-Joli, where we were relieved to reunite with Lynn after her solo cycling adventure. Sheepishly, she admitted that on her own she had gotten lost several times and inadvertently once found herself on a controlled access highway, where the Quebec police picked her up and drove her to a safer road. By morning, the previous day's tailwind holiday was gone, forcing us to face strong headwinds on a 99-kilometre grind to our next campground, called Motel de l'Anse, just a few kilometres west of Rimouski. Although the wind stilled by evening, the overnight chill turned into a torrential downpour. Until this point, we had mostly had good luck with rain – we encountered very little until we reached eastern Ontario, and even then the rains were gentle and reasonably warm. Often, they would coincidentally come on days we have booked off for rests.

At Rimouski, our luck ran out.

We woke up in the middle of the night to the sound of pelting rain and winds viciously ripping at our tents. As the winds tore stakes out of the ground, I felt the tent walls slapping my head. This was more than a downpour; it was a deluge. Most of our five tents withstood the wicked winds and relentless rain well. Lisa had wisely chosen high ground for our tent. Colleen's tent sat in a low spot but miraculously the waterproof floor kept the interior dry. Andy suffered a much worse fate – his tent collapsed at about 5 a.m., forcing him to shelter in the nearby washroom for the rest of the night.

"I thought we should have had a contest . . . the last tent standing," Lynn quipped as we ran to a picnic shelter at first light. Although her tent stayed up, her clothing got wet. As we stood shivering under the shelter, watching the rain drive down in sheets, I turned to our leader Rick. With a look of resignation, he simply said, "We're taking a rain day." It seemed to be the worst possible time for Lisa to resume full-time riding, but there was no backing out now. Andy had to head home to Christie Lake. The plan was for him to drive to Ottawa in the van, and we would fly there and pick it up when we finished the ride. Lisa's first full day back on the ride would be one of the worst weather days we encountered during the entire trip.

But kindness knows no provincial boundaries. Lisa found an Airbnb just a few kilometres down the road. When we messaged the host, Jo'Anne Roberge, at 10 a.m. describing our dilemma, she instantly replied, "Come now!" She even gave up her own bedroom so four of us could stay at her home. As she prepared to head into her job as a server at a local restaurant, she asked how we would get around town. We had no idea. "If you drive me to work, you can have my car," she said.

Lisa, Jo'Anne, Doug, Colleen

Sitting on the south shore of St. Lawrence, Rimouski is a mid-sized town (slightly less than 50,000 people live there) that faces the river. Not surprisingly, the dominant structure downtown is a Catholic church – St. Germain Cathedral, the mother church for the Roman Catholic Archdiocese of Rimouski which stretches all the way east to the tip of the Gaspe Peninsula. The diocese is one of the oldest in Canada, reaching back more than 150 years. Institutional reminders of the church's historical influence are scattered throughout the city, with more than a dozen churches, convents and presbyteries throughout the immediate area.

A modest town, Rimouski is touched by the folksy charm that makes the Gaspesie such a delightful place to visit. After a day of relaxing in downtown cafes, drying clothes and tinkering with bikes, we picked up Jo'Anne from work – only to find she brought with her gourmet-style mac-and-cheese dinners from the restaurant for us. We thought we had rented an Airbnb, but in fact, we had found a rent-a-mom. Exchanging heartfelt hugs in the morning, we struck out under a welcome sun for the last stop on our magical Quebec tour. With clearing skies in the morning, we rode along the St. Lawrence, watching the north shore recede as the river widens toward the sea. After tracing the gently curving shoreline for about an hour, feasting on the broad bays with rocks exposed by low tide, we turned inland at Mont-Joli. At Val-Brillant, we set up on a beautiful campground beside Lac Matapedia. Naturally, it was in the shadow of the old church in centre-ville, Eglise Saint-Pierre-du-Lac. To us, it was a beautiful and fitting way to wrap up one of our favourite stages of the ride.

11. NEW BRUNSWICK

THE LAND OF FOUR-WHEELED BIKES

It's a short 24-kilometre hop along Route 132 into Campbellton, a picturesque New Brunswick town that sits on the provincial border where the Restigouche River flows into Chaleur Bay. Just before we rode onto the big bridge into town, we passed by the charred remains of Saint-Anne's Catholic Church. The stone-and-wood church, built in 1912, had been the largest and tallest structure in the centre of the Listuguj Mi'gmaq First Nation until it burned in April 2021. The cause of the fire was not released by the time I wrote this, but many believe it was arson. I wondered about the mixed feelings the Mi'gmaq people must have for the church. Since the first church was built in 1771, four different buildings have fallen victim to arson.

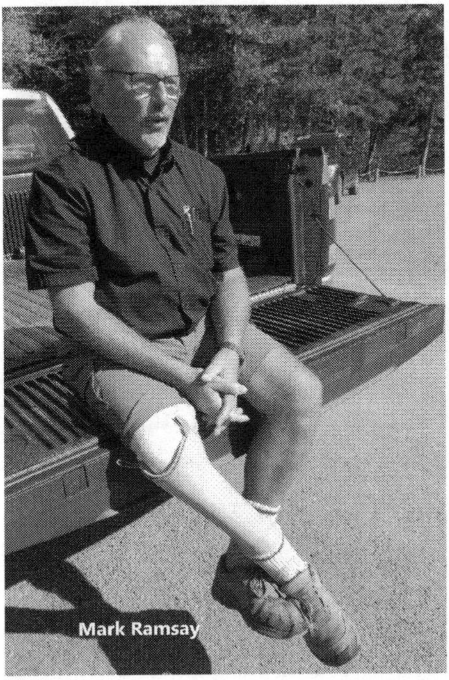

In Campbellton, we stopped in to visit owner Fred Daigle at ProX Sports, the local bike shop, and then headed in the rain for Sugarloaf Provincial Park, where we planned to camp and rest for a day. The multi-use park has a lovely, wooded campground, hiking trails, downhill biking in summer and skiing in winter. I found assistant park manager Mark Ramsay to see what all the fuss is about. Born and raised on the northern edge of Acadian New Brunswick, Mark took a break from directing traffic at the annual Terry Fox Walk/Run which just happened to be going on that day. "It's a hidden gem," Ramsay said of Sugarloaf. "We live in a beautiful area."

Beautiful, yes, but an area that has faced some of the same economic challenges that many cities and towns in the Atlantic Region have had to deal with. Once a thriving industrial town with more than 12,000 residents, a series of economic blows have hit the community hard. They include major cutbacks at the Intercolonial Railway (a CN division) and the closing (followed by partial reopening) of the mill in the adjacent village of Atholville that provided hundreds of jobs. When the Intercontinental Railway was reorganized in the mid-1970s, nearly 1,200 jobs were lost, and many families left the area in search of employment elsewhere. With the forestry sector also experiencing a downturn, it is estimated $50 million was lost from the payroll.

Today, the population in Campbellton has fallen to about 6,600 people, almost half of its peak.

Senior governments have tried to help ease the transition, but Ramsay is critical of their handout approach. "When I was mayor, I used to tell the government, 'Don't just give us money and walk away.'" First elected to council in 1999, Ramsay began two terms as mayor in 2001 (ending in 2008). He and his wife also raised a family of three, and now have three grandchildren. Among the highlights of his time in office was seeing the city host the Canada Winter Games in 2003, which created a legacy that endured for years. One of them is Sugarloaf itself, a park just two minutes' drive from town and where an annual pass is just $250.

A ski hill in New Brunswick? I ask. "We get 15 feet of snow here, naturally," Ramsay replied.

After running a fishing camp for several years, Ramsay worked for New Brunswick Tourism in 2005 before joining Sugarloaf. It's a big job in a town small enough that everyone knows your name.

Ramsay has not ruled out a return to politics one day but, in the meantime, he'll just continue to enjoy this place he has called home his whole life. "I love the outdoors. We live in a beautiful area," he says. I asked him what the one thing is that he would tell people about why he stays in Campbellton. "It's the people," he says without hesitation. "We live here because we want to live here. We have the best of both worlds."

The next day, Sept. 20, is federal election day but the outcome is not top of mind for us. Instead, we are focused on the coastline we traced along the Chaleur Bay to Bathurst, where we found Warmshowers hosts Dustin and Meaghan Dahn, and their two boys, Elliott and Mason. We camped in their treed backyard and watched while the boys picked up the rooster running freely around the yard. The next day, we traveled to Miramachi where we were confronted by the Miramachi Bridge, which towers 73 metres over the river. When I tried to ride onto the two-lane bridge, I was assaulted by an onslaught of honks and shouted warnings to get off the road. The message was hostile but justified. My presence on the busy bridge would have not only choked traffic but also made me vulnerable to an intense crosswind. Instead, we precariously walked our bikes single file across the one-kilometre bridge on a metre-wide concrete sidewalk with cars brushing by us as we grasped the railing to keep from being blown onto the road.

We were rewarded on the far side of town with a welcome from Warmshowers host James Tremblay. As we set up our tents, James ordered us pizza and we sat up until dark drinking beers and telling tales from the road. In the morning, we carried on James' tradition of having guests sign the wall in his garage bathroom while James made us a hearty egg breakfast.

We were now deep into Acadian country in this, the only bilingual province in Canada. My elementary school education never included even a mention of the heartbreaking tragedy of Acadie, as more than three centuries ago the region became the political football for two European powers battling to control the colonies of North America. Although European traders and fishermen had visited the area, it wasn't until 1604 that a French presence was established. Over the next few years, Acadian settlements spread across the Atlantic region. But over two decades of fighting, ownership of the Acadian colonies flipped back and forth between the French and English.

The Treaty of Utrecht ended the War of Spanish Succession in 1713, making the Acadians in Nova Scotia permanent British subjects, while what is now Cape Breton and Prince Edward Island remained French. The British demanded that Acadians sign an oath of allegiance to the British Crown that included a pledge to fight against the French. When most of them refused,

British Governor Charles Lawrence ordered the Acadians deported and their homes and barns burned. Many families lost everything they owned in this, the Grand Derangement. The expelled Acadians ended up in the New England states and as far south as Georgia. By the end of the hostilities, an estimated 10,000 to 18,000 Acadians were expelled and thousands more were killed.

In 1763, France signed the Treaty of Paris, ceding its North American colonies to Great Britain, except the islands of St. Pierre and Miquelon, which remain French today. With peace at last, Acadians slowly began to return to the region. Others, however, settled in Louisiana, and their descendants, the Cajuns, have kept their language and lifestyle alive.

The tragic history of the Acadian people was captured in Evangeline, an epic story by American poet Henry Wadsworth Longfellow. His melodramatic description echoed in my mind:

This is the forest primeval; but where are the hearts that beneath it
Leaped like the roe, when he hears in the woodland the voice of the huntsman?
Where is the thatch-roofed village, the home of Acadian farmers,
Men whose lives glided on like rivers that water the woodlands,
Darkened by shadows of earth, but reflecting an image of heaven?

Today, most of Canada's 500,000 Acadians live in New Brunswick, P.E.I. and Nova Scotia. Their culture is being studied and nurtured at l'Universite de Moncton, the largest Francophone higher educational institution outside of Quebec. In December 2003, fully four centuries after the founding of the Acadie, the federal government agreed to issue a proclamation in the name of the Queen recognizing the wrongs the Acadians suffered during the deportations of the Grand Derangement.

As we rode along the coastal roads, massive red, white and blue flags with a yellow star, blow defiantly in the wind, declaring these proud and hardy people are here to stay. That evening, we camped near Bouctouche at Vins de l'Acadie, a winery and campground owned by Denise Boucher and Serge Maury. Denise told us the couple bought the farm the winery sits on in 1994, a year after they were married. Their kids, now in their 20s, run the winery and campground. The family creates about 8,000 bottles each year of summer wines from locally grown grapes – Marichal foche, elderberry and blueberry.

It is a beautiful campground, but the mosquitoes are among the most voracious we have encountered in the entire ride. Weren't these things supposed to be worst in Manitoba? Not this trip. And things had gotten complicated for one of our riders. Lynn, our go-it-alone cyclist, developed an agonizing saddle sore. After battling it for a couple of weeks, she finally admitted that she could not continue the ride. That day, Ray Quan had joined us from St. John, N.B. His wife, who drove him to our rendezvous, volunteered to take Lynn to St. John to seek medical treatment. On the edge of tears, Lynn left us behind vowing to return. But we later learned that her open wound was so bad that she had to return home to Alberta, much to the relief of her husband, Grizz.

In the morning, hounded by mosquitoes we packed up early and headed out for a 98-kilometre ride to Murray Corner, which will put us minutes away from the Confederation Bridge and our next province – Prince Edward Island. Along the way, we stopped at Shediac for a less-than-satisfying traditional lobster roll lunch. It's one of those times we wished we knew where the locals, rather than the tourists, ate. The provincial campground at Murray Corner was closed but the caretaker of a nearby private campground welcomed us. "I've got a bike, too," he said, and took us over to show us what a New Brunswick "bike" looks like – we call them side-by-side ATVs.

It's a bike. Really.

To spare us from the mosquitoes, he opened up a massive shed, which had plenty of room for sleeping bags and also happened to have a great kitchen and fridge. God bless him! Only Rick, the most experienced traveler, chose to set up his tent outside.

12. PRINCE EDWARD ISLAND

A HAIL MARY TO SAVE HISTORY

I had long dreamt of riding my bicycle across the 13-kilometre Confederation Bridge. Three or four years earlier, Lisa and I had joyfully ridden a motorcycle across this massive span during an East Coast tour with two other couples. But we learned that bicycles are not considered safe on the bridge, with the passage's unpredictable wind patterns. Instead, we loaded up our bikes on a trailer and then took a taxi across. Yet it was one of those moments when we couldn't believe our good fortune. When we started the trip, the East Coast provinces were under the

"Atlantic bubble" – meaning no visitors would be allowed in. By the time we got there, those restrictions had eased somewhat, although we still had to undergo a COVID test before P.E.I. would allow us in.

Like everything else in Atlantic Canada, the capital city of Charlottetown is miniscule by the standards of the rest of Canada. A mere 36,000 people live there – and yet we recall from elementary social studies that it carries outsize importance in Confederation. A centrepiece is Province House, the site of the Charlottetown Conference of 1864 that laid the groundwork for the forming of our nation three years later. Our host for the first evening there was Jennifer Keenan, a friend of a friend who was ready to show us some P.E.I. hospitality. In fact, she turned over her entire downtown flat to us, forcing her to sleep at a friend's place. The next morning, when Jennifer returned, she introduced us to Paul Coles, her neighbour across the street – someone who has devoted his life to preserving the city's historical architecture. We learned that he's living in one of his greatest achievements.

Paul's small house in the historic downtown Hillsborough district has a modest exterior of dark red wooden cladding, making it easy to dismiss as cute but insignificant. Under that cladding, however, is an historic log house built in 1844. It is, in fact, the third oldest known log home in the city.

Paul Coles in his cabin.

It was also at the centre of a controversy that saw it damaged and nearly razed by its previous owner who was rebelling against the city's historic designation that brought with it tight controls on renovations. Then-owner Ray Campbell was so determined to get his way with the city that he deliberately made a hole in the house's roof, and took a chainsaw to some of the logs at the house's corners in the hope it would collapse. Apoplectic city officials threatened heavy fines if Campbell continued.

Then, in 2018, Paul stepped in. He runs a small heritage home renovation business. In addition to working for clients, he has bought, renovated and sold about 20 properties in Charlottetown over the past two decades. So, when he heard the old log cabin was in peril, he offered to buy it, not as an investment, but to be his own home.

"The previous owner was an anti-establishment drama guy," says Paul, grinning as he recalled the difficult negotiations to take over the cherished house. "I've bought and sold some 20 properties; this was the worst closing I've ever had."

It was also a sign of the challenge Coles, 55, faced as he planned how to restore the building while adding modern conveniences. He started by bringing in a friend who was an expert in restoring logs, and who is knowledgeable in dendrochronology – determining a log's age by studying its rings. The friend cleaned and refinished the logs and replaced the ancient chinking with modern material.

Coles decided to expose the log walls inside while adding insulation and wiring on the outside of the building, which was then covered by new wood cladding. While some purists object to not seeing logs on the outside, Coles says it was common 100-plus years ago to cover the exterior to prevent the logs from rotting. Because the house was moved one lot east onto an uneven foundation in 1923, it has a distinct tilt to it. One corner of the house sits a full 15 centimetres lower than the far corner, Coles said. "At the end of the day, I wish I had disassembled the whole house and built a new foundation."

Renovations included replacing the rear half of the roof to add more room on the second floor, adding a steel beam to reinforce the structure and replacing the joists under the entire main floor. Tiled sections of the floor have in-floor heating. Still, much of the home's original charm remains, including the worn pine floorboards on the second floor. The kitchen area has been opened up, but – as with much of the house – materials from other houses have been repurposed to keep the time-period feel. The kitchen cabinets, for example, are clad in wainscotting taken from an old church, and a reclaimed window on an interior wall overlooks the staircase.

The exposed logs display the craftsmanship of the time, says Coles, when there were no mass-produced nails to hold the structure together. Instead, the structure is held together through wooden pegs and dovetail joints. The central chimney – which once vented a large hearth – has a tilt of about 10 degrees. Coles says tilting chimneys were common at the time, built so the chimney exited at the roof's peak.

As recently as 20 years ago, the neighbourhood the house sits in was a notorious bootlegging part of the city. It was only cleaned up after a local MLA drove the charge for a crackdown on the illegal activity. "Ten years ago, no one would come down these streets," said Keenan.

Coles has won eight City of Charlottetown Heritage Awards for his restoration work, which includes another nearby house that dates to 1810. But it turns out he likes old things in general, including classic cars. He owns a 1952 Studebaker pickup truck, an original Datsun (now Nissan) 240Z sports car and Corvette Stingray, both from 1993.

The next day we woke up to a steady rain, but a friend of ours offered us the use of her CRV. Ray, Lisa and I drove out to Greenwich Prince Edward Island National Park on the north shore. We walked in the mist to the near-deserted beach pondering how romantically lonely life must be on this island. By the time we returned to an Airbnb we had rented in Charlottetown, we discovered that Jennifer's friend Aubrey had brought us a mess of freshly caught cod to feast on.

By morning, the skies were clear and we headed out on a secondary road to the Woods Island ferry that will take us to

Nova Scotia.

Throughout the trip, the riders for the most part have gotten along remarkably well. This day wasn't one of them. In fact, it was a terrible day for Lisa and me, and it was my fault. Lisa was still feeling tenderness from her collarbone and was riding slowly and cautiously. As I held back to ride with her, I felt my frustration growing. Eventually, I blurted out, "Come on, Lisa. You're riding like a turtle." My cutting remark, which I immediately regretted, set off a furious response that cast a pall on the rest of the morning and our 45-minute ride across the Northumberland Strait to Caribou, N.S.

13. NOVA SCOTIA

A COLD AND WET TURNING POINT

The chill didn't ease until we rode into Pictou late afternoon looking for a campsite for the night. There, our spirits were uplifted by Cameron MacDonald, the amiable operator of Harbour Light Campground, a private RV park that faces Pictou Harbour.

"I haven't seen bikers in two years," MacDonald said. "You're not going to pay anything tonight and I'm buying you supper." An hour later, several pizzas arrived at our campsites.

That evening, Rick and I walked out on the spit called Lowdon's Beach. A decommissioned wood mill in the distance was the only blemish on a sweeping natural vista, dotted with a handful

of lights on the distant shore as evening closed in. Now nearing the end of September, we were aware of how the shorter days were adding urgency to complete the trip. Soon, the rains will become more regular and the temperatures much colder.

It rained again overnight, and we packed up in humid conditions. As we rode through New Glasgow past the idled paper mill, I thought of it as a metaphor for the entire Atlantic provinces. Seat of the European conquest of North America, the East Coast enjoyed many decades of prosperity and industrial activity as we exploited resources on land and in the sea. But as the resources ran low and populations migrated west, the prosperity gradually wound down into an enduring economic malaise. Recent interest in the area's cheap housing has drawn both Canadians and Europeans back, and yet mementoes of those earlier ages dot the landscape like old scars from a barroom brawl.

We rode along gently rolling roads until we were forced onto Highway 403, the Trans-Canada, for a section. Halfway to Antigonish, we jumped onto the much quieter Highway 4 which runs parallel to the Trans-Canada into town. Yet even these pastoral side roads are not without danger.

As Lisa and I rounded a curve, a tractor-trailer pulled out to go by us. Just about the moment it pulled up beside us, another tractor-trailer came charging from the opposite direction. "Take the shoulder! Take the shoulder!" I shouted to Lisa, and we both did, with me rolling into the ditch. We were unhurt but angry as I had been after the near-miss in northern Ontario. If I could get my hands on that driver . . .

To our surprise, as we rounded the next bend we found the truck stopped and waiting for us to catch up. "Are you all right?" said the driver, clearly distraught by the incident. I felt my anger dissipate as he apologized profusely for his error in judgment. He promised to radio other truckers on the road to look out for us. Damn! I could not stay mad.

Rolling into Antigonish, we were hoping we could book one of the trailers at the Widden's Campground right downtown, but the operator told us they had all been leased to students attending nearby St. Francis Xavier University.

Ray Quan

We had no choice but to set up and prepare for another wet night.

Fortunately, Rick the veteran had a massive tarp that we stretched over the picnic table and a couple of the tents. We found comfort in a local brew pub called Candid and crawled into our tents to endure another hard overnight rain.

THE DAY WE ALMOST QUIT

It was cold and miserable as we packed up in the morning and set out on a planned ride of 110 kilometres. Before the trip, a friend of mine told me you cannot expect to wait out every rain and still make progress. When it rains, you ride. We folded up our soaked gear with grim determination, telling ourselves the sun would be back at some point during the day. These are the lies you must embrace sometimes to keep moving.

The rain did lighten a bit as headed toward the Canso Causeway, the link between Nova Scotia's mainland and Cape Breton Island. Just short of the causeway, at Aulds Cove, we let the rest of the crew ride ahead as Lisa and I stopped to meet with my cousin Debbie and a former co-worker of ours, Mary MacKay. We hadn't seen Mary in 23 years, and she seemed joyful to spend time with us over lunch. After lunch, Debbie and Mary pointed out that it could be hazardous to ride across the two-lane causeway in the rain so they offered to be our escorts, driving behind us to hold up traffic. As we headed across the causeway as quickly as we could, we could hear horns honking from impatient drivers behind us, and we couldn't help but laugh at the royal treatment we were getting from our two friends. From there, however, the ride through Port Hawkesbury and on to St. Peter's via Highway 4 was a cold, miserable ordeal that took us longer than we had planned. It was 6 p.m. and getting dark by the time we rolled into Joyce's Motel just past the town on Bras d'Or Lake.

Shivering as we stripped off our soaked clothes, Lisa and I huddled in our cabin and contemplated our future. The past couple of days had tested our spirits. Lisa and I were feeling emotional fatigue from our time on the road, and we were at a pivot point. If we are this cold and wet now, what will Newfoundland be like? Looking at the map, we realized it would be a relatively short hop from our motel back to Halifax. Could we ride there and declare that we had completed our goal of riding across Canada? Perhaps.

But then again, perhaps not. When we told Rick of our desire to abbreviate the trip, a hint of disappointment crept into his eyes, betraying his poker-face. Finally, he spoke: "You are certainly free to quit at any time," he said to us, and then he paused for a couple of minutes. "But I thought the plan when we set out was to ride to St. John's."

We looked at each other with resigned grins. Was there any doubt that we would be going to St. John's?

It was the right – or at least, fortuitous – decision. We didn't know it at the time, but we had ridden through the worst weather of the trip. And while the road to St. John's was no walk in the park, it wasn't the nightmarish ordeal we feared. In fact, more serendipitous rewards lay ahead.

Warming To Newfoundland

The next day's ride to North Sydney, where we would take the ferry, was a not-insignificant 103 kilometres. The skies were lightening as we left the cabin at St. Peter's, but the entire morning involved riding up and down fairly steep rises. Ray's energy was flagging and his bike's shifting cable frayed, forcing a stop for repairs. By 1 p.m., Ray, Lisa and I were all tired and ready to break for lunch, while Colleen and Rick rode ahead. We stopped near Ben Eoin Provincial Park, pulled the tent out to dry and saw a woman walking out of the woods toward us.

Cheryl Sampson told us she lives in Saskatoon but grew up on the land we were lunching on and likes to come back for visits. Though retired, she decided she would not move back to Cape Breton because she hated the mosquitoes (Amen, Cheryl) and long, wet winters.

We caught up to Rick and Colleen at a little fish-and-chip shop called Chip 'n Dales and then carried on into Sydney first, where we parted with Ray who was headed back to New Brunswick, and then to North Sydney. Our ferry was booked for the morning, so we camped at nearby Sydney Mines. The camp operator told us we were in luck; it was traditional music night at the Blue Mist Tavern. It was an authentic East Coast evening, as four local fiddlers, a piano player and one woman playing a Bodhran (Irish drum) calmly, almost stoically, worked through a long list of East Coast standards throughout the evening.

Next stop: Province #10. The profundity of this last leg of the trip was sinking in. But first we faced a six-hour ferry ride across the Cabot Strait to The Rock. For me, it was also a chance to find out what kind of person pilots the MV Atlantic Vision, the massive ferry between these two great provinces. Once we were sailing, I passed a message through a staff person to the captain. Would he talk to a crazy cyclist who's keeping a journal of our trip? Within a half-hour, I received a message that Capt. Stan Peet had the time to sit down with me. We started by talking about his own roots in Atlantic Canada. Capt. Peet was the youngest of five children when he was born in Nova Scotia's Annapolis Valley, yet he feels as much a Newfoundlander as his siblings who were all born on the island.

And like all true Newfoundlanders, he said he believes his home province is every bit as much a distinct society, with its culture and heritage born from its isolation, as Quebec is.

"We are a very proud group of people," he said, as we gazed out over the waters. "We are definitely part of Canada, but we are a distinct society."

Capt. Stan Peet on the bridge.

The 203-metre-long MV Atlantic Vision is the largest passenger ferry in North America, and it makes the daily six-hour trip between North Sydney, N.S., and Port-Aux-Basques, NL. It was the jewel in four-vessel Marine Atlantic fleet when the Crown corporation acquired it in 2008. Built in 2002 in Kiel, Germany, it was one of just a handful of vessels that met the criteria Marine Atlantic required when it was shopping for a ferry.

Peet was among the team that selected the ship, and he was put in charge when it sailed out of port in Finland, when the company took possession. What he hadn't figured on was that he would be the one to steer the massive vessel out of the European country's narrow and unfamiliar fjords. "It was interesting to say the least," he says, his eyebrows rising at the memory of the trial by fire.

Although he had decades of experience commanding large ships, including supertankers for Irving Oil, he said every vessel behaves a little differently. "It's just knowing the feel of the ship," he said.

Compounding the challenge was the need to adjust direction to compensate for wind currents that can blow a ship into rocks with little warning. With its 4,300 square metres of surface area on the side, the Atlantic Vision is "like having a massive piece of plywood in the wind."

Although he got out of the port in Finland, the challenge of getting the vessel safely across the Atlantic wasn't over. In the English Channel, the ship encountered a "big storm" with nine-metre waves that tore the ramp off the top deck.

"It was a pain in the ass," said Peet. "I'd been up for, at this point, 24 hours. When I did finally get back to the cabin, a cupboard door was laying on my bunk."

These days, the sailing is much smoother. The company does not sail on days when waves exceed five metres or winds exceed 30 knots (56 km/h). This is especially important sailing into Port-Aux-Basques, where the channel is so narrow there is little room for error.

"You're seconds away from – if you make the wrong manoeuvre – getting out (on the rocks)," he said. He can recall at least one very close call over the years. Although two newer vessels in the fleet can handle more than the Atlantic Vision's 350-car volume, it remains an impressive vessel. Powered by four 16-cylinder engines, it sends 62,000 horsepower to its twin propellers. Its hull is also rugged enough to sail through Atlantic ice. On at least one occasion, it helped free an ocean liner that had become ice-bound, Peet said.

Peet maintains a close relationship with his crew of 69 (in mid-summer, it swells to 100) and believes in treating everyone on staff as an equal. "I'm no more important than the purser," he said, "Or the person who will clean the decks. We don't put ourselves above each other."

At age 59, he could retire, but he enjoys what he's doing and wants to stay for at least another five years. For two weeks at a time, he oversees two sailings – one around noon, and the return trip at midnight. Yet, despite the demanding hours, he is happy with the work/life balance, because he gets two weeks off for every two he works. When he's home with his wife Janis, he loves to spend days on his personal sailboat.

Peet says separatists, like some in Quebec, who want to go it alone would do well to travel the world and see the state of other countries. It would help them appreciate what they have here, he says.

"Canada is a good country. We are very fortunate."

Peet took me up into the bridge to study the high-tech navigation gear, and then invited me back up there to watch the delicate docking in Port-aux-Basques. I didn't make it back because by the time we docked it was getting dark and we had to get off the boat and to our Airbnb for the night. Unfortunately, on our way across the strait, the Newfoundland and Labrador government tweaked its Covid documentation requirements for anyone entering the province. Hundreds of cars and five bicycles leaving the ferry were held up for hours while each of us struggled with downloading a new app. By the time we made it to our shelter, it was pitch black and, once again, the streets were slick from rain.

14. NEWFOUNDLAND

HIGHWAY MOTELS CLING TO THE PAST

It is now October – the fickle month of, at times, "Indian summers" as we used to call them and, at others, glimpses of winter. There is one way, and only one, to get from Port-aux-Basques to St. John's. It's 900 kilometres along the Trans-Canada Highway. The only shortcut is a section of logging road, but descriptions made it sound barely passable on heavily loaded bikes – all to save about 50 kilometres of distance. Thinking back to our hellish "shortcut" in Ontario, we didn't give the logging road a moment's thought.

The streets of Port-aux-Basques were still wet, but the sky

was mixed as we started the long trek along the Trans-Canada Highway to our final destination. A few kilometres out of Port-Aux-Basques I saw a sign that read "St. John's 890 km," and my heart sank. I felt a sudden melancholy wash over me as I realized the end of our odyssey was in sight. This trip had become much more than a life-transforming journey; it was now our way of living. We weren't riding bikes to get somewhere; we were riding because that is what we do.

Our day's ride was easy, with gently rolling hills and light traffic. To our right was the stunning Table Mountains and to our left the vast ocean. It was like being dropped into another planet. We quickly learned that October cycling in Newfoundland has one major drawback for campers: Virtually every campground is closed and there are few good spots for rough camping. So, this evening our destination was literally the only place to stop for 100 kilometres – the Midway Motel, so named for its location halfway between Port-Aux-Basques and Corner Brook. There, we found Norm Noseworthy and Diane MacDonald. That evening, as we finished supper in the empty lounge, they told us the motel used to be a thriving business when the area's population was bigger. Diane's parents had a gas station, garage, restaurant, convenience store and the motel. They said the lounge at the motel was often full. But as people moved away, and the patriarch died (and a brother died when a rubber dingy sunk), the mother was unable to sustain the business and it gradually dried up.

Lisa picks up the story:

Diane was raised on 'the highway' after her parents bought the land and opened a gas station and the motel in 1954. She took it over

after her parents died. She tells us there's no place she'd rather live. "I feel comfortable here," she says. "It's home."

The Midway was once a hopping place with weekend dances, bar fights and other shenanigans with the locals. But many people have moved away and the hotel's mainstay is overnighters from the ferry traffic from Port-aux-Basques. The couple recently sold the hotel to another family member and they have plans to spruce it up and reopen the restaurant. Norm and Diane will stay and operate it.

For the ConnecTour gang, the Midway was like an oasis in the desert on a rainy and cold night. We used a stove sitting in the idle lounge to make dinner and then our hosts regaled us with tales about living in Newfoundland – including one story of being blown off the highway by the crazy winds while Norm was driving a passenger bus. Remarkably, everyone survived.

The next morning, we loaded up and began the 108-kilometre ride to Corner Brook. If there's one thing this trip has taught me to hate, it's the spray from passing trucks. The rain had stopped in the morning, but there was plenty of moisture on the pavement waiting to be q

hurled at us from the tires of the massive haulers that roared past at times close enough to be in arm's reach. Truck spray is shitty for a lot of reasons. It's dirty – so filthy – picking up the dust, tire particles and occasionally the essence of animal guts from the road. It showers your face in a fine mist forcing you to squeeze your lips together in a vain attempt to avoid ingesting any of the detritus. It sprays your clothes and eventually leaves you a sogging, stinking mess. The only good thing about it is that it eventually stops. It was a constant drizzle around 1 p.m., when a clearly hangry Lisa demanded we stop for lunch.

But where? There were no rest stops or picnic tables anywhere on the route; we eventually found a gravel turn-off where we could huddle and make lunch. By late morning, the pavement had dried up and we enjoyed intermittent sun as we pedaled across constant ups and downs. (There was quite of bit of elevation change that day – 1,266 metres). By late afternoon, we reached Corner Brook and rolled down very steep streets to our cozy Airbnb. My rear wheel, I later learned, was slowly disintegrating and I had to squeeze the brake lever with all my might to keep the heavy bike under control on the steep grades. Losing the ability to slow down with a fully loaded bike is a bit terrifying. At the Airbnb, I put new brake pads on in the hopes they would improve my stopping power. The Airbnb was heavenly, with heated tile floors in the kitchen to take the chill off. Nobody felt like cooking that night, so we ordered pizza and hit bed early.

Of course, in the morning we had to climb up those same hills. After a kilometre of exhausting work, we reached the Trans-Canada, and the road leveled out as we traversed through the Humber River valley and past the Marble Mountain ski resort. The trees had taken on the fall brilliant reds and yellows and we laconically made our way to Deer Lake.

The next day was to be a longish one, with our destination of the Junction Inn motel near Baie Verte just shy of 100 k. The fall colours were settling into their full glory, and the ride along Deer Lake was stunning. However, when we arrived at our motel, we discovered that not only was it ugly and junky on the outside, but, even worse, it was also closed for the season. We pondered camping on the site, but there was no access to water or electricity. We decided to ride 24 more kilometres to the Burnt Berry Motel, not knowing what it would be like or even being certain it was open.

I was tired and frustrated and rode that distance as fast as I could, with only Rick able to keep my pace. Yet, a minor miracle lay ahead. About halfway there, I spotted a large bull moose by the side of the road ahead of me. I had expected northern Ontario and other locations to be overrun with these animals, and yet this was the first and only one I saw. As a truck approached from the opposite direction, the moose (thankfully) ran up the embankment and into the woods.

The Burnt Berry was modest in a way only rural motels can be, but it had its own charms. It had a Coca Cola themed diner, and waitresses dressed in period outfits. I took a long bath and then looked at my pathetic bicycle seat. Rick and Tanya had bought a used leather seat for me in Winnipeg, trying to win me over to the Brooks cult. This B17, however, was ancient and the dried-out leather had torn in two in the past couple of days. I stuffed a spare tube under the seat and wrapped the whole thing in – what else? – duct tape. That, I figured, would be enough to get me to St. John's. When Rick saw my McGyver, he looked on with a mix of fascination and horror. Did I really want to subject my ass to that? Fortunately, four months and 8,500 kilometres of riding toughens up a butt pretty well.

Doug's 'repaired' Brooks bike seat.

After downing a beer in the diner, we decided we'd take a pass on the uninspiring menu offerings, and made dinner in our room, which happened to be equipped with a stove.

The next morning, as we set out for Grand Falls-Windsor at 8 a.m., the intense cold stiffened up my aching fingers so much I could barely grip the handlebars. My feet were also intensely cold and I didn't know whether I could stand it. Gradually, the day warmed up as we came across beautiful Baie Verte, a deep fjord that flows out to the ocean.

A couple of hours later, we stopped for lunch in a little hamlet called Badger, population of about 700. Way back in 1992, Chatelaine magazine had named it one of North America's top communities to live in, but I was having a hard time figuring out how they arrived at that decision.

We had lunch at a park named after Ted Patey, a local broadcasting legend. Displays in the park told the story of the Shawadidinth and the Mi'kmaq people. And there was a long piece on the misfortunes of the Beotuk, an Indigenous people who were killed off by tuberculosis. At Grand Falls, we arrived at our Airbnb, and discovered an overgrown yard, with stinging nettles growing out of the sagging staircase on the back deck. We made dinner at the house and watched a horrible movie, called The Kitchen, about the wives of New York gangsters in Hell's Kitchen in the 1970s who operate their husbands' rackets after the men are locked up in prison. The chance to actually watch a movie on this bike ride was so rare, it seemed a shame to waste the luxury on this crap. But that wasn't the only target of our critical eye. Rick, who is normally loathe to criticize, wrote a scathing review of the Airbnb – a place that could have been welcoming but was instead dying of neglect.

We had made it through the first week of October with remarkably friendly weather. In the morning, we headed out for our third long ride in a row. The early fall sun warmed the gently rising and falling roads and we were carried by the wind at our backs. Halfway to our destination, we stopped for lunch at an old rail bridge in Appleton. Several ATVs came by as Rick, Doug and Lisa stood on the bridge, soaking up the sun. Colleen had gone ahead to the Airbnb.

In Gander, we grabbed at beer at the Friends lounge and got a recommendation to have the burger at the Legends Lounge – a welcome break from our campsite cooking. Like so many Newfoundland services, the bar had a feel of faded glory to it, a hangover from the days when Gander served as a stopover for international air travellers. The walls were decorated with photos of musical and movie legends who surely had never actually been there. I gave in to a dare to have a Gander twist on poutine: fries, gravy and – wait for it – stuffing. There are no regrets, as long there is Pepto Bismol.

Our weather luck continued the next day. It was a planned rest day, and it was one of the days in which we avoided having to ride in a rain that set in early afternoon and stayed steady until late evening. Earlier in the day, I cycled over to the North Atlantic Aviation Museum and interviewed Sandra Seaward, a lifelong Newfoundland resident and museum CEO.

She told me that, although she grew up just an hour from what was once one of North America's most important airports, she didn't have much of an interest in studying its past. "I never had an affiliation for history," she says, scrunching her face into a frown. "It had a lot to do with my history teacher in high school."

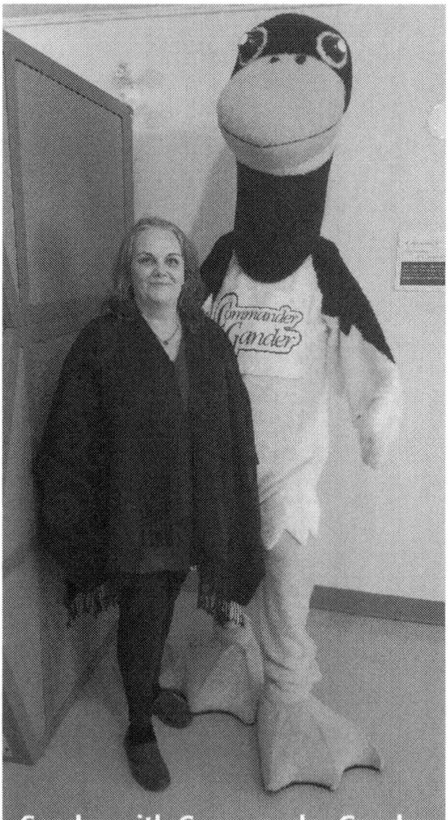

Sandra with Commander Gander

That all changed in 2013, when she was recruited to be CEO of the museum. Although she was hired on the strength of her administrative skills, she quickly found herself immersed in the fascinating series of events that both gave this small city on the northeastern side of Newfoundland its identity and juiced its once-booming economy.

She has also had the opportunity to meet some of the unsung heroes involved in the top-secret Ferry Command project that helped change the course of the Second World War. Two of those unsung heroes were women – Hazel Fausak and Gloria Lindsay. Hazel, who died at age 92 in 2016, did encryption for Ferry Command and Gloria did inputting. After the war, the women were simply sent home, without an honour or a pension to compensate for their contributions. It wasn't until 2015, when the museum held a gala to celebrate the 75th anniversary of Ferry Command, that the two women were reunited and given acknowledgment for their contribution to the war effort.

Ferry Command was created in response to Britain's desperate need for aircraft in 1940, when the Nazis superior air power seemed insurmountable. Seaward says ships carrying aircraft across the ocean were often sunk, and – even when they avoided such a terrible fate – it could take as much as three months to ship the aircraft overseas. But what if the aircraft could be flown over?

The British War Ministry decided to try flying the aircraft to Britain, using the Gander Airport as the jumping-off point. The first trip in November 1940 involved seven Lockheed Hudson bombers, and the crew were offered the then-enormous sum of $1,000 if they arrived successfully.

"They all made it," says Seaward, and that success "popped the cork" on Ferry Command. By the end of the war, about 10,000 aircraft had been ferried by air from Gander.

"It made a huge difference," says Seaward. "It definitely changed the course of the war."

Gander's aviation history predates the war. The little town was hand-picked for greatness during the nascent days of cross-Atlantic passenger air travel. British Overseas Airways Corporation was building air mail and passenger routes, and hired an aviator named Col. Doug Fraser to find an ideal location for aircraft travelling from the U.K. to refuel. He chose Gander in 1935 for its absence of fog, favourable winds and proximity to easily identifiable Gander Lake. By 1938, the world's largest airport was in full operation.

"Then the war broke out," says Seawater. According to an apocryphal story, Adolf Hitler so hated the strategic value of the airport to the Allies, he had a standing order to destroy it. "But," says Seawater, "they couldn't find it."

The war had a huge impact on the town, with as many as 15,000 people working at the airport.

After the war, before aircraft developed longer range capabilities, the Gander Airport was known as Crossroads of the World. Celebrities who stopped there include Elvis, Marilyn Monroe, Jackie Kennedy Onassis, Winston Churchill, John Wayne, Frank Sinatra, James Dean and Soviet cosmonaut Juri Gagarin. "It wouldn't matter who it was; they had to stop here," says Seaward. It was also considered a neutral ground during the height of the Cold War. On New Year's Eve in 1972, Cuba's Fidel Castro famously borrowed a young boy's toboggan and tried it out during a trip through the community.

But as transatlantic flights no longer needed to stop to refuel, traffic in the airport declined. By 1961, just 5,700 people lived in town, although the population has since grown to nearly 12,000 today.

Two more recent events have seared Gander into the world's

psyche.

The first was a devastating crash of Arrow Air Flight 1285R, which was carrying U.S. troops from Cairo, Egypt, back to Kentucky. On Dec. 12, 1985, the plane went down shortly after takeoff from Gander, killing all 248 passengers and eight crew members. It remains the deadliest crash in Canada's history. Seaward's husband, Greg Seaward, was working for the local newspaper and was the first photographer on the scene.

"He saw some pretty horrific sites," says Sandra. "Decapitated people, the smell of burning flesh and burning jet fuel."

An investigation by the Canadian Aviation Safety Board concluded the probable cause of the crash was reduced lift, caused by ice on the wing's leading edges and upper surfaces. It also stated the plane's weight was underestimated. But a dissenting report from four of the nine investigators challenged that theory and speculated that an onboard fire of "unknown origin" was behind the crash. Seaward says many Gander residents still believe there was a coverup behind the tragedy. Several residents reported seeing flames coming from the plane while it was still in the air, and one resident says he heard a loud thump.

The other event was more positive and is celebrated in the hit Broadway musical *Come From Away*. During the Sept. 11, 2001, terrorist attacks, a number of passenger flights were diverted to Gander. Within three hours, air traffic controllers at Gander had commanded 42 aircraft to land and got them on the ground safely. "There was not as much as a nicked wing," says Seaward. Controllers "did an absolutely phenomenal job."

How the town responded – with food, accommodations, and gifts for 6,700 unexpected guests – is a matter of national pride. Years later, Seaward was invited to Manhattan to watch the musical on Broadway.

These days, the museum is working to raise as much as $5 million to build a hangar large enough to bring their beloved Lockheed Hudson Bomber aircraft indoors, where it can be preserved. It sits outdoors, and Seaward says it is slowly eroding in the elements. Only six of the aircraft exist in the world, and the one at Gander is the only one in the Americas.

It's a machine that tells the story of the people involved in the war effort, says Seaward, who was involved in bringing the plane to the museum from a podium it sat on adjacent to the airport.

"When I saw that plane on the highway, I knew it had to come to town."

The next morning, we took flight via peddle-power from Gander en route to Glovertown, riding in a light mist. Within an hour, the rain had stopped, although the clouds hung overhead. It was a short day – just 64 kilometres – and we got to town before 1 p.m. Finding most of the town closed down (on a Saturday!) we hiked up to a lookout, which provided an overview of the town and bay.

The next morning, we faced a steep climb out of Glovertown to the Trans-Canada, a preview to the challenging hills as we passed Terra Nova National Park.

And then catastrophe struck. Well, pretty small scale to some of the disasters we'd already experienced. Right beside the Terra Nova visitors centre, I had my first flat of the trip. A big ol' rusty nail, like hundreds I had dodged during the ride, found its way into my seemingly indestructible Schwalbe Marathon Plus tire (you're welcome, Schwalbe). Looking up, I saw Rick in the distance halfway up the next hill. Rick, with the good tire pump. Reluctantly, I called his number for help. As I explained my dilemma, I heard a sigh and then a long pause. Surely, Rick was thinking I could manage this on my own (which, truth be told, I could have, given enough time). But there was a biting wind and I hated the idea of having to pump hundreds of strokes on my underpowered tire pump to get to useable tire pressure. The nail had gone through the tread and came out the sidewall – potentially compromising the tire. But a little duct tape provided the extra support. Within minutes, we were back on the road. The skies slowly cleared as the day progressed, and by early afternoon we were able to start shedding layers. The hills became gentler as we approached our destination at Hillview, a house at the top of a steep hill by Queens Cove.

No, Not What You Think

I won't kid you. We were influenced by some juvenile impulse to ride to Dildo the next day so we could photograph ourselves by the sign. How many thousands of tourists have done the same thing? I wonder. Stupid mainlanders that we are, we didn't know that the term dildo describes the little brass pin that serves as the pivot point for the oar in a rowboat. Over the years, local residents have wrestled with renaming the community, but ultimately have decided to keep the name. I'm glad they have.

The trip is just two days from ending. We can't believe it. That evening, as we sat around the dinner table in our cute little Keeting Cottage Airbnb, we talked about what the trip had meant to us. I flipped on the GoPro and recorded our feelings for posterity.

“This trip has just been fantastic. Nothing’s really gone wrong,” said Colleen. “I feel happy, sad, apprehensive – everything all at the same time.” (As it happens, just that day Rick had to use his mechanical wizardry to fix a broken shifter cable on Colleen’s bike. When we couldn’t find the spare shifter cable that we had packed deeply into our gear, Rick modified a brake cable to do the job. Those with bike mechanical experience will know just how remarkable an achievement that is. That day actually became quite serendipitous. While Rick and I worked on Colleen’s bike, Lisa rode ahead to an Irving gas station a few kilometres up the road. By the time Rick, Colleen and I got there, we were greeted by a group of kayakers who Lisa had befriended. Learning of our adventure, they greeted us like rock stars. And one friendly man, Pat Dornan, gave me his card and told me that if we needed anything at all in St. John’s, just give him a call.)

Rick was next. “I’m happy that we’re going to be in St. John’s,” he said. “That was the goal. Originally, we said Halifax and you (Doug) said, ‘Wait! Why not St. John’s?’”

Oh yeah, I did that, didn’t I?

“I am blown away by the fact we’re actually here,” said Lisa. “I have gone in and out on a trip that I never thought I would be a part of. . . . I feel like I have become a completely different person by being able to finish this.”

“If you had asked two years ago if I’d be cycling across Canada, up massive hills, I would never have believed I could do anything of the sort." Her co-riders, she said, have given her the power to carry on.

I was the last of the four to speak. "The trip has changed me in really fundamentally, basic ways," I told the group. "I've met so many people who I admire and love . . . I just think it's been the greatest experience of my life."

The ride the next morning from Keeting Cottage was relatively easy but getting into St. John's was not. As we fought our way up several hills, we were buffeted by crosswinds in bone-chilling cold. The misty rain in the 7 C air looked like light snow, adding to our discomfort. We exited onto a city street and rolled downhill about 20 minutes to downtown. Lisa and I met up with Rick and Colleen at the Yellowbelly brewpub and quietly celebrated our accomplishment over a beer. A drunken cyclist from Ireland approached us and regaled us with stories of his own travels. But, when we spotted him the next day, he didn't recognize us. Oh, beer. We capped the day with a visit to the Terry Fox memorial at St. John's Harbour.

The next day we were greeted by the lovely and gracious Sheilagh O'Leary, deputy mayor of St. John's.

Our official greeter, Sheilagh O'Leary, left, at City Hall.

"What a feat it is that you've done," she told us. We talked about the "wild times" the country had experienced because of the COVID pandemic and the impact on our sense of connectedness, especially in Newfoundland, which has higher levels of isolation.

"It's been tough," she said, noting that she founded the annual Tickle Swim in 2013 to raise awareness and reduce stigma around mental illness.

"I highly commend the work that you've done in order to bring people together," she said. "It's human nature. We need to connect. It's so important."

"It really does help to the bring bar up, just a little bit in terms of letting people know, 'You know what? We're still here. We can still connect.'

"As a society, we need to pull together and just be kind to one another," O'Leary said. "If we can do that, then I think our connections will bring us to a better time."

This One's For Sid

Our trip was done, but it wasn't. We had unfinished business for our friend Sid Reid, whom we had met way back in June in Innisfail, Alberta. We had promised him we would travel to Bell Island and have a beer at Dick's (pronounced Dicks-es) Pub.

It was raining the day we planned to head to Bell Island, so we scrapped our plan to cycle to the ferry dock. On a whim, I texted Pat Dornan, the man we met just outside of St. John's, to ask for a ride to the dock. Within 15 minutes, his car pulled up in front of our rental.

"I took the day off," he told us. As an RCMP officer, he had banked up more overtime than he knew how to use. "I'm going to Bell Island with you."

Teresita and Des

It's a short, 20-minute, ride from the dock at Portugal Cove over to Bell Island, a little piece of eastern Canada off Newfoundland's Conception Bay.

There, we were met by Teresita and Des McCarthy, who live on the island, and met for coffee while we planned our tour. Teresita runs the Bell Island Community Museum, so she and Des were well-equipped to reveal the island's fascinating history.

The McCarthys told us that Bell Island is one of the few parts of our country that was attacked during the Second World War, and the only domestic location where Canadians lost their lives during the global conflict.

The year was 1942, and German U-boat submarines were wreaking havoc on the East Coast in both Canada and the U.S. That year alone, the Germans sank 39 ships. Bell Island, on Newfoundland's Avalon Peninsula, became a target for the submarines because the DOSCO iron ore mine at the island's town of Wabana was a major source of raw material used to produce the war machines the Allies so desperately needed.

In two separate attacks, on Sept. 5th and Nov. 2nd, 1942, German U boats sank four ore carriers anchored off Bell Island, killing 70 merchant mariners. The ships were the SS Saganaga, SS Lord Strathcona, SS P.L.M. 27, and SS Rose Castle. Another torpedo missed the 3,000-ton collier Anna T and exploded when it hit the DOSCO loading pier. Even today, at low tide, relics of the sunken ships can be seen. Scuba divers come from around the world to explore them.

We drove to the Seamen's Memorial, at Lance Cove at the southern end of the nine-kilometre-long island. Created in 1994 by Branch 18 of the Royal Canadian Legion, it is a modest site that overlooks the scene of the U boat attack.

Teresita and Des both grew up on the island and remember the island's heyday in the 1960s while the mine was operating at full tilt. Back then, Teresita says, 14,000 people lived on Bell Island and enjoyed many of the conveniences of a large city.

"It was absolutely, positively incredible," said Teresita.

Des said the amenities included Sears and Eatons stores, a bowling alley, 13 schools, a racetrack and many churches. Workers were well paid, he said, and they "wanted for nothing."

"People would go into a store (on the mainland) with a $50 bill," said Des. "And the clerk would say, 'You must be from Bell Island.'"

Des remembers as a kid playing in the mine shafts. Like his wife, his dad and many relatives were miners. He chose instead to pursue a career as a teacher.

Teresita runs the Bell Island Community Museum, which sits at the entrance of the long-idled Wabana mine shaft #2. Though tours are suspended during the COVID-19 pandemic, we were invited in for a look. Amongst the collection of memorabilia is a map that shows a massive labyrinth of shafts and rooms that extend about five kilometres out under the ocean.

Though the shafts are now flooded with ocean water, Teresita says there is plenty of ore that could be mined. Yet, geo-economics sent this island's only industry to the dustbin of history. The mine was rendered uneconomic by cheaper producers elsewhere in the world. After years of decline, it closed its doors in 1966 – driving a stake into the economic heart of the island. At one point after the mine closed, then-Premier Joey Smallwood was seeking to remove abandoned buildings and offered to pay $1,500 to each owner of a home on the island, on the condition they tear it down. Today, 2,500 people – about one-sixth of the peak population – live there, and many commute to work on the mainland.

With Smallwood's initiative, many of the landmark buildings no longer exist.

Teresita has dreams of one day reviving the island's economy through tourism. Though it is not as spectacular as such well-known sites as Signal Hill or Cape Spear, there is much charm to be found on Bell Island. During our one-day tour, we got to most of them: the historic lighthouse; the murals that recall the island's history; the Grebe's Nest birding area, where flocks of starlings fly from nearby fields to nests located in the cliffs; the war memorials; the tunnel to a hidden beach created for the once-active fishing industry, and the memorial to the miners who died in accidents over the years.

"We have a beautiful history," says Teresita. "It's colourful and it's sad."

As we munched on local fish and chips and a brew at Dick's Lounge, we mused on an island shaped by its past, searching for a future. And we raised a glass for Sid.

15. WHAT DID IT ALL MEAN?

WHAT WE LEARNED FROM THE ADVENTURE

We had travelled 8,749 kilometres in total over 141 days on the road. Ninety nights of camping, and other nights as guests with local hosts or at hotels and Airbnbs. As a group of as many as nine riders, at times, to as few as three, we had met countless Canadians, made new friends, and explored regions we otherwise would never have gotten to in our lifetimes. And now, we had one more trip to make – the 75 kilometres from our home in Calgary to Irricana, to reconnect with Sid and Louise Reid.

Lisa and I didn't get back to Irricana for three years, and when we did it was a disappointment. Rolling into the campground on our bikes one summer afternoon, we stopped someone on a riding lawnmower and asked where could find the Reids. "I don't know them," he said. "Are they the ones that used to run the campground?"

The Reids had retired – and we didn't know whether it was for Sid's health or just because they had their fill. We were told they have moved to Calgary but numerous attempts to locate them had failed. Sid, if you read this, I hope you will know we did indeed raise a glass in your honour at Dick's Pub.

* * *

And so, our great adventure is done: 90 days camping, 14 riders, off-and-on, countless campfire stories, heat, rain, wind and unending companionship. Some of the riders who had left us along the way reached out with congratulations:

Lynn Martel (who rode with us to New Brunswick): "I am so proud of you guys, I know that it hasn't been easy and the only way you could accomplish this huge achievement is by having a great attitude. Great Job"

Tanya McFerrin (who rode with us to Montreal): "You all are awesome! So good to hear your thoughts on your adventure. Perfect timing. THANK YOU!!! Hurray! You did it!!!!"

Andy Williamson (who rode to Rimouski): "Spectacular accomplishment, with you on every turn and every climb on the Rock. Hope to ride with all of you again some other time and place down the road...."

John Singleton (my high school buddy): Congratulations to you all. You were willing to challenge yourselves and each other. Thank you for inspiring us all. Well done!

Liz Tomkins (who subsequently completed on a multi-year vanlife adventure with husband Remy): "Way to go guys! We have been following every step of the way and are so incredibly proud of you all. Having just driven a very similar route I can attest to what an incredible feat it is to have cycled it. We are in awe. Enjoy all the celebrations!"

Doug Reid (who rode with us in northern Ontario): "Crikey! What an accomplishment! You guys, along with Tanya and Lynn, are my heroes! Thank you so much for letting me join you for a small portion of your epic journey. I hope we ride again."

Laura (one of the kayakers we met at the Irving rest stop in Newfoundland): "Congrats to all of you on such an epic adventure. Great to have met you at the Goobies rest stop yesterday. Now about that screech-in!"

Jo King (who with her husband Phil met us in Nelson): "Congratulations! Amazing accomplishment. All the things the rest of us have done and have been doing since you passed through Nelson, and you have been cycling, day in day out, through that whole time!"

Reality Has Never Felt So Unreal

Returning home to Calgary after months of living a different life on the road felt surreal. It was a bit like being caught in the Matrix; one reality dissolves into another, leaving you wondering which one you can rely on.

The house was unchanged but looked foreign to us. A neighbour's daughter had lived in our house, taking care of the dog while we were on the road. Our dog, Anouk, looked at us like we had been out for the afternoon and then brought us a ball to throw. The neighbours wanted to catch us up on the gossip. We unloaded our filthy, road-beaten bikes and lovingly rolled them into the garage, awaiting the day when they'd get a thorough going-over. Nothing seemed to be quite where we'd expect it to be in the shower.

Lisa and I looked at each, happy, sad, bewildered, tired, energized. At loose ends.

What did we accomplish? What did we learn? What would be different about our lives now? What will we do differently? Will our fate be to bore our friends with endless tales of things that meant so much to us but maybe not to them?

And . . . when will we hit the road again?

I asked the ConnecTour core team to reflect on their experiences, with the highs and lows. Here's a little of what they wrote.

RICK McFERRIN:

It was a long journey with incredible experiences and lasting friendships. The idea was to cross Canada at the "speed of life" to reconnect, restore, and rebuild a sense of community after months of disruption that has come with the COVID-19 pandemic. Highlights for me included:

- The generosity of all the people we met along the way.

- The incredible diversity of Canada's landscape.
- Being active and living outdoors for 4 1/2 months.
- Sharing a way of life with others that Tanya and I have become accustomed to.

Challenging moments:

- Head winds and heat across the prairies.
- Lisa's broken collarbone crash that sidelined her for several weeks
- Riding the Trans Canada Highway when alternate routes were not possible through some areas.

TANYA McFERRIN

I have bike-toured thousands of kilometres and love the rhythm of the road and the everything about being connected to a bike. I was 51 years old when I joined ConnecTour in Calgary, and rode to Montreal. Two months. ConnecTour was envisioned by a team of like-souls and joined by numerous partners in camaraderie and commitment to travel by two wheels. I felt lucky to have been on such an adventure with such neat people.

My experience riding and living with this team as we cycled through the miles eastward across Canada had a profound impact on my soul and on my connection to Canadians as a whole. As we traveled across the country, I felt a deepening closeness to my country and the inhabitants of the innumerable tiny little Canadian towns.

In the morning, I would daily take a 15-minute pre-dawn walk from our campsite, following a nearby pathway or street. I would quietly absorb a garden of gnomes, an avenue of trees, or an odd, out-of-place architectural monstrosity in an otherwise common neighbourhood. I would imagine the people who had created these spaces. By day on the ride, I would consider the diggers of the dugouts across Manitoba, the farmers who had driven the tractors, planting the rows upon rows of billowing yellow canola, and the workers who had piled up that refuse pile of scrap metal and erected the corrugated stock tanks against which my bicycle leaned while I took a break from the road.

By evening, ConnecTour was often hosted by local campgrounds. One campground owner opened the "closed due to Covid" common room to give us a sheltered space when the afternoon raincloud settled in. Another evening, a Quebecois host gave us an amazing musical concert in the kitchen of his welcoming 200-year-old home while we used this same space to conjure up a feast for us all.

The people we met in our journey shared their lives and hospitality with us again and again. Individual Canadians shared pieces of their Canada, while their interest in our journey allowed us to share our experiences with them.

The ConnecTour had the effect it was designed to. Canadians connected with Canadians again and again across the country. Canada was shaking free the bonds of Covid and opening to a oneness and cross-country connection. On this ride, I took in Canada at the speed of a bike, with my ears listening and my eyes wide open. Upon completion, I feel accomplishment and confidence that the persons I meet, wherever I ride, support my desire to learn through experience. I am indebted to these, my compatriots on the road.

When I think about the ride, I smile, I think about sweat, I think about shared memories. The struggle of the wind and the road, the pleasure of riding as a member of a team, knowing that my team had my back. There would be the end of the day, the meetup, the sharing of stories and the feeling of exaltation at the triumph of another successful day. I think about the deliciousness of an IPA or a sour, discovered within the cooler of a small town's liquor shelf, the change out of the sweaty bike gear and the pleasure of settling down in my fold-up camp chair and catching the breeze in the shade of a building, wall or shrub.

Life on the road is pretty simple. Take care of your body, feed your soul with hours of personal one-on-one bike time, hydrate, smile and laugh. Life on the road is gold. That is what I think about when I think about this ride.

ALLISON FLACH:

My initial dream of riding my bicycle across Canada was motivated by an early pandemic restlessness coupled with a persistent hunger for open roads and unknown places. As the nebulous "two weeks to curb the spread" (of Covid) ticked on into the late spring, summer, and finally winter, wistful notions of cruising on two wheels through South America were carefully tucked away with my passport. Like many of the quarantined, my attention narrowed — to the familiar and undiscovered places of my Alberta home and the roads leading beyond.

I absolutely love bike-packing; it feeds my soul and fills me up. I love waking up outside, the smell of coffee brewing over the camp stove, packing everything I genuinely need into four bags, and pedalling off, never knowing exactly where we'll sleep. At the end of the day, when we find camp and descend from our saddles, we begin the ritual of setting up home for the night;

tents up, clothes rinsed and on the line, and a beer to mark the occasion. We prepare and eat dinner as a family, busying our hands while we share our reflections and musings of the day. It's an experience of daily ritual and community that settles the restless spirit, body, and mind.

When I joined the ConnecTour crew as they passed through Calgary in late June, I was unaware of the personal depth the upcoming journey would have. It had been just over a month since I experienced my second pregnancy loss in less than a year. Early loss is complicated; when a physical death occurs, we have rituals to process the loss and grieving is a communal experience. The disenfranchised grief I felt left me lost with what I can only explain as a sense of disembodiment, temporarily disconnected from the person I had known myself to be.

Adverse experiences leave a visceral imprint on our bodies and minds, triggering our mammalian brains to rely on defence mechanisms. We disconnect from our bodies in an attempt to preserve ourselves from pain. The path forward relies on learning to heal and rebuild, to re-connect and re-establish ownership of our bodies and our whole person. Since then, I've gained confidence in my own resilience, rebuilt trust in my body, and have become acquainted with a changed and assured version of myself.

I've always understood bicycles to be tools of self-exploration and development. Over the thousands of kilometres I pedalled that summer, I know that my bicycle served as a conduit to rediscovering my strength and self.

Everyone who rides a bike knows that cycling is good for the mood. It has the healing effect of a ritual, placing you in the moment; that magical space where movement and consciousness collide, senses are heightened, time slows down, and fears evaporate into effortless momentum. Every day in the saddle offers hours of solitude to sit with your thoughts and move through them. And yet, your crew will be waiting for you at the next rest stop and remind you that you're never truly alone. Bike trips create bonds of shared experience that foster a feeling of belonging while allowing each individual to find purpose and meaning. The empowerment brought by conquering distances, hills, weather, and mental blocks reconnected me to my inner and physical strength, to what brought me joy, and to the importance of surrounding myself with people I love.

I believe that community is at the heart of everything. As we pedalled through a heavy heatwave, down dusty roads and unfamiliar towns, I came to understand that the sense of belonging and connection I was feeling went beyond my ConnecTour family.

As strangers welcomed us into their homes, offered us food, water and shelter, or simply an encouraging thumbs up, I was reminded of the simple truth that people are kind beyond measure. As humans, we're wired to thrive in strong communities. When we move through deep struggle or loss, it can feel as if our world is crashing in. Travelling by bike allowed me to feel the vastness of the world again, and to experience the good nature of humanity in a way that wouldn't be possible through the windows of cars or motel rooms. In the months following the trip, I would go on to experience another loss.

I believe I was able to face that time with strength, resilience, and the knowledge my sense of self would emerge intact on the other side. As I moved through it, I never forgot the importance of staying connected to the community and spaces where I found belonging and support. Today, I am four months away from expecting a healthy baby girl and am already planning her first trip on two wheels. (Editor's note: Allison is now the mother of a beautiful girl named Juniper.)

LISA MONFORTON

If you'd asked me five years ago whether I ever pictured myself pedalling a loaded-down bike across Canada, I would have asked, what are you smoking? Yes, I love to travel and ride a bicycle, but putting those two passions together for an 8,700 km ride over four-and-a-half months, my brain (never mind my body) would never have entertained the idea.

But here's what I've learned in my 60 years. The people you meet in your life and your travels can have a such powerful and positive, life-changing influence on you – like getting you to say, 'Of course, why can't I do this.'

When I started the ride, I had a wee bit of bike-packing experience from a 12-day tour in Argentina with Rick McFerrin's OnaVelo company. Yes, I did get the bike-packing bug on that trip and my husband Doug and I started planning more trips like it.

When Rick first floated the idea of cycling across Canada. I demurred. What is this crazy talk, I was thinking as my husband, Doug, had us virtually signed up immediately. Flash forward 15 months later: We had amassed all the necessary gear, hashed out the route and were revved up to embark on this epic adventure. To say that I was nervous starting out on the ride is an understatement. Though I was shaking inside, I look at a picture of myself at that moment and I'm pedalling and wearing a huge grin.

I've never been one to fully embrace the "take-one-day-at-a-time mantra." I do love spontaneity, but my more reserved side also likes to know a little of what my day holds, a little certainty. But when you're travelling by bike across a vast country, you cannot predict what is going to happen in even the next moment or seconds. Is that car or semi-truck going to give me enough space? Will we find a decent place to camp tonight? And more realistically, will I be able to make it to the top of that 1000-metre hill/mountain pass?

As the days rolled by, something magical happened: my brain and body got into a well-oiled groove. I stopped worrying about all those what-if distractions. I learned a lot about myself: I am resilient, adaptable, and physically stronger than I ever knew I could be. I learned to love the unknowns of where we would be sleeping or what we were having for dinner. The beauty was in the simplicity of life: waking up after the best sleeps ever, breaking down camp, having coffee and breakfast, loading up the bikes and riding for five or six hours, buying groceries for the next 24 hours, making dinner, enjoying a couple of cold beers and talking about the day, heading blissfully tired into the tent for a 10- or 11-hour sleep.

But the real beauty each and every day was about the people we met. Strangers for whom I am forever grateful and feel so lucky to have met. Every day I was blown away by the generosity of our fellow Canadians. This is something I'd never experienced before. And it was not until I put myself out there on a bike with only the daily necessities that I found out just how kind and welcoming Canadians are. Every day, a kindness was shown to us by perfect strangers. There are too many encounters to count.

There was Ian, who, on a scorching 40 C day near Keremeos, B.C., voiced his idea of being Canadian. He brought us jugs of water and bags of ice. He had initially eyed us up with suspicion as he drove by. But then walked up to us while we were having lunch under the shade of a tree and said: "I thought to myself, I need to do something. I'm a Canadian."

On another searing hot day in the tiny town of Chinook, Alberta, Hank saw us sprawled on the grass in a slice of shade at a community centre and became alarmed. He, too, brought us bottles of water and told us to come to his yard and cool down with his yard hose. We took him up on his kind offer. Moments later his neighbour, Rick, came over and offered his yard up as a campsite and invited us to use his above-ground pool, bringing us gin and tonics while we splashed in the water. They fed us burgers in their air-conditioned barn and we gathered with his family. It was a moment I will never forget.

Outlook, Saskatchewan, was a scary and disappointing turning point for me in the ride. I had a fluky but nasty crash riding along the highway. A couple stopped to help, and after the ambulance came, took our bikes to their nearby home for safekeeping. They brought our fellow riders back to their farm for lunch while I was treated at a hospital in Saskatoon. It took a few weeks, but I fully recovered from a broken collar bone and concussion and rejoined the ride in Quebec.

It's hard for me to describe what compelled me to want to complete the ride. But I woke up one morning in Windsor, Ont., where I was recovering at my mother's, and just knew I had to get back out there. I hatched a plan to buy a used van so I could play a support vehicle role until I was ready to ride again. The day I met up with my husband Doug and Rick and Tanya in Tobermory, Ontario, was like a scene from a movie. There were tears of happiness.

I still think about it nearly every day and Doug and I talk about it often.

It's still hard for me to believe that I completed the trip which brought such serendipitous and incredible experiences. Close friends ask me how the ride changed me. I have a whole new sense of who I am and what I'm capable of. And a whole new respect for humankind.

ME (DOUG)

Yeah. All of that. Everything my close friends have had to say. The magic of knowing that the people around you are working together as a team, willing to do whatever is needed to ensure you are safe and with them. Willing to lay down their lives, if necessary – thankfully, never required – to protect the others. Confidantes. Brothers and sisters. Entertainers. Chefs (well, cooks). Mechanics, when needed. You name it.

We set out to take the pulse of Canadians, and we got it. Even in a time of crisis – perhaps especially in a time of crisis – we found people everywhere who were willing to put aside their fears of a pandemic we did not yet fully understand to be kind, generous and accommodating.

Let's be clear: There were also some jerks. There was the reckless driver who nearly mowed me down in northern Ontario. There was a cynical retiree who asked us, "How bored do you have to be to want to ride your bicycles across Canada?" There were people who told us we had no right to be on the road because when you ride a bicycle you don't pay road tax through your fuel purchase. (Hmmm, seems I also put a lot of fuel in my truck.) There was the campground owner who told us there was "no room" for us even as were standing with him, looking at an unoccupied lot. The woman who had to bleach a picnic table in front of her motel, after we stopped there to lunch one day. There were the idiot drivers who honked at us and motioned at us to move onto dangerously loose gravel shoulders. Yeah, Canada is not Pleasantville writ large.

Everyone has pain in their lives. Sometimes, that manifests itself in open hostility, sometimes in depression or withdrawal. We saw people like that. Others look for rays of sunshine in spite of the things that have gone wrong for them. They care about others more than they do about their fight with the neighbours.

Some of the people we met described this phenomenon as being Canadian. I like that idea; that we see ourselves as caring people, like all those families in Gander who turned a massive invasion of international travellers into a huge kitchen party.

We all know Canada is an incredibly massive country. Seeing it by bicycle drives home just how big and diverse this land is. From the rugged Rockies to the sun-baked prairies to Ontario's Canadian shield, Quebec's pastoral farmland and Atlantic Canada's maritime magic, we travelled through regions that at times seemed to evolve hour by hour, even at 18 kilometres per hour. It you can't find a part of this country you'd want to spend the rest of your life in, then you are very picky indeed. And, yes, I know our tour didn't even touch on the North, a project for another day.

Lisa and I have travelled by bike to several countries since our cross-Canada ride. In every country we've been in, we've found good people. But there still seems to be something unique about the Canadian brand of kindness. Is it because we are still a relatively new nation? Because we remember that many of us have come from other countries looking to build a better society here? I don't know, but I hope we never lose it.

I hate the things we are seeing from our so-called leaders today. Prime ministers and premiers who talk as though they've never sat down and had a beer with a real Canadian in their entire lives. People who are too willing to give in to influences that drag us down. People who live in border cities who know more about the murder rate in Detroit than they do about what's going on in Tuktoyaktuk, and know the temperature in Fahrenheit but not our own standard. We're better than that. It seems the further away you get from the U.S. border, the more you find people who have true sense of what makes Us different from Them.

Canada. You're all right. But you've got work to do. Thank you for opening your doors to a handful of scraggly strangers and showing us what makes us who we are. The gift you have given us is priceless.

Canada Is Worth Fighting For

When we started the ride across this incredibly diverse and beautiful nation, we had no idea of the turmoil Canada would come to face in a few short years. The country next door – the one we assumed would always be a reliable ally – has turned on Canada, thanks to its narcissistic leader. Donald Trump and his sycophants continuously question why the border between our two countries even exists. He's openly expressed his desire to fulfil the United States' dream of Manifest Destiny, in which the entire continent is absorbed into his troubled nation.

The people who would subdue us through conquest know little about our country, what drives us, what we stand for and what we value. Although Canadians have struggled with persistent internal conflicts driven by regional resentments, as our group cycled across the country, we were struck instead by how much more we have in common than what divides us. In every province we touched – and we touched them all – we were greeted by people with open hearts, good humour and genuine hospitality. These generous people fueled our belief that those nagging regional differences could somehow be overcome if we just engaged as one Canadian to another.

It's been so easy for so many years, it seems we got too comfortable as a nation. We came to rely on the U.S. for military defence and economic prosperity. We got careless with our finances and became smug over the institutions – like universal health care – we claim make us morally superior. But the political sucker-punch from a man who represents the worst of our southern neighbour has woken us from our slumber and brought us closer together. There's nothing like an existential threat to focus the mind. It has reminded us of why Canada is worth fighting for.

There's one other thing the people who would subdue us don't understand: Canadians have iron wills and stiff spines. Our polite nature masks a toughness underneath. If you want to challenge us, insult us, and take a broadaxe to our economy, get ready for a fight fiercer than you ever could have imagined. We know more than ever that we live in a very special place, and we will do whatever it takes to protect it from external forces that want to take us down.

Elbows up. If you're not Canadian, you probably don't even know what that means. But if you want to threaten us, you're going to find out.

Footnote: Dax Gets A Second Liver

The life-saving liver transplant that son-in-law Dax received was not ideal. He was given a less-than-perfect match because his health was declining rapidly and something had to be done quickly. But over the coming months he fought frequent complications, including recurring infections in a drain port that was needed.

In early March 2025, Dax received a second liver transplant. This

one seems to be a far better match and his recovery is going well. We thought we were pretty brave to cycle across the country but his journey – and the support of his dedicated spouse, Lauren – required so much more courage than ours.
We are delighted to see that he is finally on course for many healthy years ahead. Miracles come in many forms; this one came thanks to the unrelenting efforts of the medical staff at Vancouver General Hospital, to whom we are forever grateful.

And the miracle did not bankrupt the family. Publicly funded health care may not be perfect, but the fact that such care was within reach undoubtedly saved Dax's life.

16. CONNECTOUR COOKBOOK

NOT QUITE GOURMET BUT NOT BAD

Several members of our group are masters of the impossible on the road. What often looked to me like a bunch of compost could be turned into a healthy, tasty meal. I marvel at the magic our group, often collectively, was able to perform on whatever we found in our food pannier at the end of they day. If necessity is the mother of invention, then this crew are innovators extraordinaire.

Here are a few of our favourite recipes from our road-side culinary explorations.

Recipes

All of these dishes can be made over a compact camp stove, using simple ingredients that travel well.

8-MINUTE PARTY DAL

Ingredients:

- 1 heaping tbsp. (20 mL) virgin coconut or olive oil
- 4 cups peeled (if necessary) and diced veggies*
- ½ cup (100 g) uncooked red lentil
- ½ cup (125 mL) water, plus more if needed
- 1 (14-ounce/398 mL) can diced tomatoes
- 1 (14-ounce/398 mL) can light coconut milk
- 1 ½ tsp (7.5 mL) garlic powder
- 1 ½ tsp (7.5 mL) minced onion**
- 1 tbsp (15 mL) good curry powder

Instructions:

1. In a large pot, melt the coconut oil over low-medium heat.
2. Peel (if necessary) and dice the veggies into ½-inch pieces. Add them into the pot and stir until combined. Increase heat to medium.
3. Add in the rest of the ingredients (lentils, water, diced tomatoes with juices, coconut milk, all the spices, salt and pepper). Stir until combined.
4. Increase heat to high and bring to a low boil. Reduce heat to medium and cook uncovered, for 18 to 30 minutes, until the veggies and lentils are tender; the cook time will depend on the types of veggies used and their size.
5. Stir the dal frequently while cooking, and reduce the heat if necessary to prevent it from sticking to the pot. (If you're using potatoes, cover the pot while cooking since they don't contain as much water to "cook off." You may need to add more water to thin the mixture.
6. If desired, serve over basmati rice and garnish with freshly chopped cilantro leaves and lime juice. (It's still delicious without these additions though!)

Veggie combos can be whatever you like: Some suggestions are carrot and zucchini, potato and peas, sweet potato and red pepper, broccoli and zucchini, cauliflower and/or broccoli.

CAMP STOVE FAJITAS

Ingredients:

Volume varies, depending how many people you are feeding and how hungry they are:

- Onions
- Jalapenos
- Sweet Red Pepper
- Protein: (I.e., Tofu, chicken, pork, beef)
- Can of black beans
- Shredded cheese of your choice

- Cilantro and hot sauce of your choice

Instructions:

1. Stir fry veggies (ie: onion, jalapenos, sweet pepper) and the protein (i.e., tofu, chicken, beef or pork)
2. Warm up flour tortillas in a frying pan.
3. Fill tortillas with contents and spoon over warm-up can of black beans Add shredded cheese, cilantro and hot sauce.

RICK'S CHEESERS

Ingredients:

- Any bread or bun, but sourdough or a hearty chewy bread is best
- Olive oil or butter
- Cheddar or a combination of any cheeses
- Salt
- Oregano (optional, garlic powder and chili flakes)

Instructions:

1. Butter or dredge bread on one side in olive oil.
2. On the buttered or oiled side, season with salt, oregano, garlic powder and chili flakes.
3. Place one slice of bread in a skillet, butter/oil side down.
4. Add several layers of cheese to the bread slice.
5. Top with the other bread slice, butter/oil side up Cook in skillet, flipping occasionally, until you have toasted, melted cheese deliciousness.

ASIAN BOWL

Ingredients:

- Grain of your choice (brown or white rice, quinoa)
- Stir-fry veggies of your choice (i.e., onion, garlic, cabbage, carrots, celery, mushrooms,
- Sweet peppers, jalapenos)

Instructions:

1. Saute veggies in a pan till cooked to your liking.
2. When almost cooked, crack an egg on top, stir and cook to your liking.
3. Serve over the cooked grain in a bowl.
4. Soy sauce is a nice add-in if you have it on hand.

SMOKED SALMON PASTA

Ingredients:

- Box of short pasta, like penne or corkscrew
- Small tub or block of cream cheese
- Package of smoked salmon sliced into ribbons or strips
- Green onions or chives
- Lemon

Instructions:

1. Cook pasta until al dente.
2. Drain pasta, keeping a small amount of water aside, or the pasta moist if that's easier. (This helps make the cream cheese creamier.)
3. Add cream cheese to pasta and stir, until creamy.
4. Add in salmon strips and stir.
5. Keep warm (although still good at room temperature) and top with green onion or chives.
6. Squeeze a bit of lemon over top to add a bit of brightness to the dish.

GREEK PASTA SALAD

Ingredients:

- Box of pasta of your choice (but a short pasta like penne or corkscrew works best)
- Sweet red pepper and green pepper
- Purple or sweet onion
- Black olives (pitted kind)
- Tomatoes (preferably fresh)
- Protein such as tuna, chicken or pork
- Feta Cheese
- Spices, like oregano and thyme, if you have on hand
- Lemon, olive oil

Instructions:

1. Cook pasta according to instructions. Set aside to cool.
2. Chop up sweet peppers and onion.
3. Toss together well chopped up sweet peppers and onion (and protein if using) with pasta, add in black olives, feta cheese.
4. Add in olive oil and stir well. Give a good squeeze of lemon and mix all together again.

ABOUT THE AUTHOR

Doug Firby

Doug started writing as a kid by long hand before he learned how to type. It was a lot of fun because when you're a kid you can say what you want without the filter of editors and other people who think they know better than you.

One day, a high school English teacher wrote on a paper Doug had submitted that his writing would one day make a difference. It was a confidence-builder, and enough to encourage him to pursue a life in words.

For decades Doug wrote and edited news stories, features, opinion articles for newspapers and magazines. But it was only after leaving the world of news media that he could once again let his thoughts run wherever they would take him.

A lifelong cycling enthusiast, Doug discovered the joy of bike touring on a recent trip through northwest Argentina led by his friend Rick's touring company, OnaVelo. "At bicycle speeds, you get a more powerful sense of place," says Doug.

A journalist, adventurer and conservationist, Doug and partner Lisa have explored parts of Canada, Central and South America and Europe and fill their weekends with cycling, kayaking, skiing, and hiking in the Rocky Mountains.

Manufactured by Amazon.ca
Bolton, ON

55596474R00146